Selling: The New Norm

Selling: The New Norm

*Dynamic New Methods for a
Competitive and Changing World*

Drew Stevens

BEP BUSINESS EXPERT PRESS

Selling: The New Norm: Dynamic New Methods for a Competitive and Changing World

First published in 2016 by
Business Expert Press, LLC
222 East 46th Street, New York, NY 10017
www.businessexpertpress.com

ISBN-13: 978-1-60649-980-1 (paperback)
ISBN-13: 978-1-60649-981-8 (e-book)

Business Expert Press Selling and Sales Force Management Collection

Collection ISSN: 2161-8909 (print)
Collection ISSN: 2161-8917 (electronic)

Cover and interior design by Exeter Premedia Services Private Ltd., Chennai, India

First edition: 2016

10 9 8 7 6 5 4 3 2 1

Printed in the United States of America.

Abstract

Why read another book on selling? Simple. Today's client is more informed, more sophisticated, and has more access to information. Selling professionals today need to be keener to fulfill the needs of the client by offering value, and most important trust. In the increasing age and rage of globalization and the Internet, competition rises. Selling professionals today need to determine better ways to reach the economic decision maker and better articulate their value. *Selling the New Norm* is such a book. This book will provide the tools and templates required to meet today's sales challenges.

Keywords

creating a sales training program, decision makers, developing a sales training program, enterprise selling, sales management activities, sales management analysis and decision making, sales management basics, sales management best practices, sales management building customer relationships and partnerships, sales management business plan, sales negotiation, sales process, sales training books, sales training ideas, sales training programs, sales training techniques, start a sales training business

Contents

Acknowledgments

Developing a work like this is no easy task and not one for any single man. There are so many people to thank along the way, but unfortunately I will somehow wind up missing someone near and dear to me and for that I apologize. However, this text would never have come about without the expressed love and support from my dearest soul mate Christine and that of my immediate family, Andrew and Ashley. Many nights they sat on the couch watching me keyboard away in trying to find solutions to bridge the gap on the lack of knowledge and the intellectual property chiropractors need.

During my many years in business, I have had mentors who have come and gone. Most recently, those who have really placed a positive effect on my business include both Alan Weiss and Rob Nixon. Alan, you have made me realize what value and articulation of value mean to clients. And Rob, you helped me understand how to package and promote my business, so that others truly understand what I bring to the table. And finally, the true inspiration to the stories, case studies, and examples in this book could not have come from a better core group than my 30 years of clients who've allowed me to serve them unquestionably over the years, while also allowing me to place a positive spin on their business and on their business future.

And finally, no author or expert could ever just thank those currently present in his or her life. My principles, my core beliefs, and my undying methods for achievement would never have been set if not for those in my adolescent years. From Anthony "Box" James, who taught me the value of looking forward and always looking at the finish line to both Golda and George Jeffrey, who taught me the value of research and self-appreciation, to finally Marney Ranani, who lit a candle to my future and blew out the candle to my dysfunctional past: all of you have continually shown me the light each and every day so that I may light the way for others and guide them to the achievements you always thought I could achieve. God bless you all!

CHAPTER 1

Inescapable Change—Why It Is Required?

The oldest and most intriguing profession in the world is selling. Since the beginning of time, Bedouins and nomads exchanged goods and services so that each could survive. As civilizations developed, selling became a much more structured platform. Various civilizations from the Romans to the Eastern European explosions developed selling into what it is today. However, it was not until the late 1920s and early 1930s that selling became an American or even international institution.

For this, we need to thank individuals such as Napoleon Hill, Zig Ziglar, and the iconic Dale Carnegie. Each of these gentlemen brought with them the passion and the education required to develop relationships with consumers. Each of their structures helps formulate the backbone of what has become the foremost recognized international profession.

As with any institutional development, changes always occur. Selling has experienced this in its 2,500 years of existence. For example, practices have altered due to uncontrollable environmental factors such as, but not limited to, political, economic, technological, legal and regulatory, competitive and social cultural. Each of these has played a vital part in altering the landscape of selling.

Much like anything else, and without sounding trite, the world of selling is once again morphing. Recent changes both technologically and economically have created a plethora of professional changes. Presently, we are undergoing shifts in the technological aspects of selling, which have drastically affected business-to-consumer and business-to-business (B2B) relationships. Additionally, we are also beginning to experience huge demographic shifts, which have impacted the manner, style, and technique in the selling environment. Finally, the worldwide recession of 2008, entitled the "Great Recession" by some, gave rise to dramatic decreases in sales training, sales management training, and even the sales focus. What we are experiencing now is being called, "The New Norm."

Technological Change

There are 2.5 billion Internet users at a global level as of beginning of 2014 (meaning 35 percent Internet penetration worldwide). Internet penetration by region: North America 81 percent, Western Europe 78 percent, Oceania 63 percent, Central and Eastern Europe 54 percent, East Asia 48 percent, South America 47 percent, Southeast Asia 25 percent, and Africa 18 percent (Peltea 2014). These numbers are quite staggering since almost 35 percent of the world uses the Internet to conduct research as well as acquire products and services. During the early days of selling, gentlemen for the most part built relationships and exchanged goods for money with direct contact. In fact, the only means of commerce was specifically meeting with individuals. It was not until the invention of the telephone and even years thereafter that altered the landscape of selling was altered so that individuals did not have to meet directly, but could offer features and benefits of the product via the telephone.

Technology has inhibited many of the relationship sales techniques of the past. For the most part, the average consumer today is conducting a majority of research on products and services. With well over 700 million websites according to Internet research and well over 1 trillion web pages, consumers have many directions to operate in determining the best fit for their needs.

What this means to the sales professional today is that the landscape has completely changed. I recall entering sales in the early 1980s, and there were numerous buzzwords such as: relationship selling, consultative selling, account management, guerrilla selling, global account management, executive account relationship, solution selling, and so on. No matter what was called, the notion was to build a relationship with the client and assist the client in making a resourceful, equitable, and robust solution to meet their needs. Notwithstanding, the customer today conducts a treasure trove of research before engaging a sales professional. In fact, a recent Corporate Executive Board study of more than 1,400 B2B customers found that those customers completed, on average, nearly

60 percent of a typical purchasing decision—researching solutions, ranking options, setting requirements, benchmarking pricing, and so on—before even having a conversation with a supplier (Adamson, Dixon, and Toman 2012).

For many years, especially during the 1980s when I first got into sales, we were always taught to provide a solution to the individual consumer. These solutions were based upon their wants and needs. In fact, a key component to something at the time was their dominant buying motive, and this was the chief reason why someone would require a product or service. I remember spending an inordinate amount of time in my Dale Carnegie training solutions classes understanding dominant buying motive in order to provide the proper solution to the consumer. However, this inferred that the average consumer was unfamiliar with a particular purview of products and services, and it was required of the sales representative to educate the consumer. In fact, back in the 1970s and even perhaps the 1980s, a selling professional was much more of an evangelist and educator rather than a solution provider.

As we can now attest, this landscape is completely altered. Consumers today are a keystroke away from understanding solutions they need or even want! With the largesse of the Internet and Internet pages, consumers today frequently know what they want prior to even engaging with some sales representative. Take for example the number of individuals that walk into a retail store with a mobile phone or tablet of a competitive product or even a competitive price. And with many products currently utilizing barcode readers, a consumer has instant access to competitive prices while in the store.

Comparatively, for the B2B sales professional, their entire platform is based upon relationship. As I mentioned previously, one of the key terms back in the 1980s was relationship selling. However, even the business consumer today is not necessarily concerned about the relationship. Corporate procurement, chief executive officers, chief information officers, and even those in middle management are concerned about one thing—profitability! Consumers desire the least expensive, the fastest alternative, and the easiest road to corporate profitability.

Much of this is attributed to the Great Recession of 2008 through 2009. Organizations in many ways, including but not limited to small businesses, were deeply impacted by the economic meltdown. As such, corporate profits and productivity significantly altered the method in which selling professionals were used, and because of the quality of the Internet in terms of price, products, services, competition, and so on, the salesperson of yesterday has become slightly disposable. Don't misunderstand me, selling professionals are still required; however, the notion of solution selling and being consultative is less important today than it was 20 to 30 years ago.

Measurements

In addition to the notion of technology, another alteration in the sales umbrella is the manner in which reporting is conducted. For the last 20 years, sales managers have formulated their meetings around the number of customers seen, the volume of sales, and the amount of revenue for each particular selling representative. However, this tended to assume that some selling professionals were farmers and some were hunters. These numbers then formulated a chasm between top achievers and mediocre. The problem with this particular model is that it always assumed that the top performers were always going to thrive, and the middle-tier performers were going to be just that or eventually cast out.

What we are seeing is a longer sales cycle and sales managers who continually use rote measurements to determine sales growth. The number of appointments, the number of calls, and the number of accounts does not equate to revenue. For example, an organization in Kansas measures its revenue opportunities based on the number of calls that the selling professional makes every day—65 calls! First, there is no way that a qualified selling professional can have a purposeful and relationship-based conversation with 65 individuals. Second, this denotes the age-old formula of cold calling and quantity calling that left the industry ages ago similar to that of door-to-door selling professionals. What needs to be measured today is output. In other words, how many qualified conversations is the selling professional having with his or her consumers. Most importantly, what is the feedback from those consumers? I'm often reminded of Steve Jobs who spent an inordinate amount of time with consumers attempting to discover their needs. Selling professionals today need to do the same.

Providing corporate executives with valuable feedback from consumers will help minimize the sales and increase revenue opportunities.

Another key area that sales managers never seem to review is actually whom the sales professional is speaking with. Too much time is spent dealing with subordinates who make no decisions. This is not to say that procurement officers and other middle managers are not important. However, there is too much wasted time today between the sales professional and subordinates who make no decisions. For the average and even best professional to thrive in today's brutally competitive corporate market, they must speak with people who make decisions. While many individuals may infer that this is the chief executive officer, it need not be. Yet, the one thing that has never really manifested is who are the best people who can cater to the consumers' desire while eliminating the sales gaps.

Consumer Buying Behavior

Sales managers and professionals also need to understand that the consumer buying behavior has altered forever. With the increase of mobile devices and consumers being attracted more toward communities that influence decisions, the need for selling professionals is different. During the last 10 to 15 years, the world has experienced the rise of organizations such as Apple, Facebook, Starbucks, TOMS Shoes, Twitter, and many others. These organizations have one intriguing thing in common, they all never advertised. Each of these organizations was able to formulate a community that supported their efforts to come up with their products and their passion. Coincidentally, it was consumers and pundits who became avatars in manifesting the brand. In most instances, selling professionals were not used. In fact, Facebook and Twitter have no sales representatives. And, Apple while it does employ technicians does not use sales professionals even in their retail establishments. These multibillion-dollar organizations all began and continue because of the passion, enthusiasm, and conviction that their individual communities have for their services.

Therefore, today's selling professional similar to these organizations needs to discover for himself or herself how to develop community. In 2008, the author Seth Godin wrote a book entitled the *Tribes: We Need You to Lead Us*, whereby he asserts that individuals can formulate communities wherever they are. These communities help to build relationships and connect people to new products, services, and ideas. Therefore, the sales representative today is no different. Every interface they have is all about building relationship. Their entire purpose is to build as many relationships as possible in order to establish value so that individuals understand that value and exchange it with money. That then is a sale.

The sales representative today is required to fully engage with as many individuals as possible to formulate as many tribes as possible. This is because the number of relationships will help to establish numerous communities that will help manifest the value that they provide. In other words, today's sales professionals are not necessarily in the sales business; they are in the relationship business. The sooner they get adjusted to that, the better it will be for future revenue growth. Discussions are not predicated on price, product, or even service. Discussions with potential community members would be about value and solutions and opportunities that you can present to them.

How might salespeople provide this, you might ask? Here are a few techniques to help develop stronger relationships and demonstrate that value, which then could result in a higher commission and higher commitment from the client.

1. Focus on the results the individual consumer desires. In fact, you might even want to pitch additional results that the consumer had not thought of. When the consumer sees you more as a valuable asset rather than as selling professional, fees no longer become an option.

2. Stop asking the same questions that any other selling professional would ask. Become a valuable part of the organization by reading its annual report and researching analyst reports and even the company website. By becoming an expert analyst you will be able to assist the organization with new solutions rather than just the one they are looking at.

3. Take the time to really listen to what the consumer is saying. Too many selling professionals want to talk and no one wants to listen anymore. Take the time to take notes and really understand what the consumer's needs are.

4. Stop talking too much and allow other consumers to provide the talking for you. In fact, this is why so many consumers tend to spend so much time on the Internet because many organizations make false claims. The only way to really establish value is by providing testimonial in case studies of other customers who received results from your current array of products and services. Believe it or not, many potential customers just want to hear from your other current customers.

5. Customer service is paramount to your organization success. This means that the front desk has to be completely available and helpful. It also means that selling professionals return calls in a timely manner. For example, I return all calls within 90 minutes of receipt. Not many other consultants can make such a claim. If you want to stand out of the crowd, you can't look like all the other chess pieces.

6. All selling professionals must understand that all purchases are emotional. Not many make pragmatic decisions. Find out what the true motives are for the decision and appeal to that emotional side.

7. Consumers want to understand, especially in a B2B environment, the value that your particular product and service can provide as well as the measurements for success. Provide the consumer with the customer testimonials available that will assist him or her to understand that value. When you hone in on value in ways that you can measure the success of your particular product or service for that organization, you will be closer to a sale.

Customer Service

The management guru Peter Drucker wrote a book many years ago entitled *The Practice of Management*. The famous work depicts a classic quote that has been used numerous times. "The purpose of business is one thing—the customer." In other words, the customer owns the business and everything happens around the customer. To Drucker, all marketing, all research, all sales, all talent acquisition, and finally all management decisions are based upon the consumer. What this should mean to any selling professional and their manager is that all decisions and actions are based upon what the customer wants.

Numerous businesses over the years have focused on this vital principle. Zappos, the online shoe company has for years offered intense customer service. For example, one customer service call lasted over six hours! The Four Seasons Hotel has provided amenities for guests over the years based upon their desires. SAS Institute hires individuals for the purpose of providing extreme customer service.

If selling is an exchange of money for value then customer service is the linchpin of that value. Nothing in the organization will ever happen without focus on customer service levels. Customers today desire responsiveness, follow-up, and professionalism. Let's look at each of the three in more detail.

Responsiveness

We all know that in today's Internet connected world between cell phones, instant messaging, and even e-mail, the conductivity from one to another is achieved in less than a second. Research has shown that delaying a follow-up call by even 30 minutes can have huge implications for your close rate. For example, during the writing of this book I have had several vendors approach for a variety of services. In the last 30 days, six vendors had appointments with me and each was late by an average of 22 minutes. None of them received the sale! Tardiness is a simple sign of insincerity. Tardiness is also a sign of disrespect in which their time is more important than mine. Unfortunately in our fast-paced competitive world, time is of the essence. And no one's time is more important than the customer's. Hence, if you want to succeed in today's world then time will be the salesperson's first degree of focus.

First and foremost in the world of B2B selling relationship is vital to success. In order for any salesperson or manager to conduct business well, any conversation with customers should be scheduled and confirmed. While a multitude of business today is secured through telephone lines, one of the worst methods for scheduling is the use of Microsoft Outlook. Too many send invitations to others without conferring if the time and date is acceptable. Coincidentally, sending an e-mail invitation is disrespectful because it assumes that the other person is responsible for scheduling the appointment. If you want to schedule a meeting with the customer, then call him or her on the phone, request an appropriate date and time, and place it on each other's schedules.

Once the appointment is scheduled then it is best to call 24 to 48 hours in advance to confirm. Most professionals attend a total of 61.8 meetings per month and research indicates that over 50 percent of this meeting time is wasted. Since there is much schedule shifting, this is a very professional way to ensure commitment. Additionally, to maintain the relationship, the confirmation must be accomplished through a phone call and not an e-mail. Too many selling professionals hide behind e-mail today; this is not only unprofessional, but also dismissive. Be professional and pick up the telephone.

Once the appointment is confirmed, the selling professional must prepare for the call and be ready to make it at least 5 to 6 minutes prior to the appointment. Too many meetings run late and this becomes disrespectful of everyone's time. There is a wonderful video on YouTube that illustrates how disruptive meetings become when people are late and fail to get attention. The video can be found at www.youtube.com/watch?v=DYu_bGbZiiQ (Crosby and Stanton 2014); assuming the meeting does happen then it is the selling professional's responsibility to ensure both goals and time of the meeting. This provides assurance to the consumer of the selling professional's desire to meet customer's expectations by not wasting time.

Finally, as the meeting concludes, proper action steps should be taken. No one should ever leave a meeting with a customer without appropriate action steps so that the customer understands how his or her expectations are met. Any lack of responsibility and follow-up will have the customer calling one of your competitors quicker than you can say your company's name.

Follow up

An overlooked area for many selling professionals is failure to follow up. Ironically, with the multitude of customer relationship management software, many selling professionals simply fail to follow up. For some, this may be due to the multitude of account responsibility. For others, it could be the intensity of the day and lack of time. And for some others, unfortunately, gross negligence. However, for any sales manager and customer, there is nothing more important than promised follow-up. In other words, if a selling professional states that he or she will call on a specific day and at a specific time, the call should be placed moments before the appointment. Follow-up calls similar to the mortgage are due on that day. Nothing is more important! Not missing a scheduled follow-up call is as important as the first call to any customer.

Furthermore, there are times when there is negligence in follow-up upon a customer connecting with the selling professional. In other words, a customer calls, leaves a message, and requests a return call. Statistics in data are unavailable to provide an appropriate example; however, based on some of the information listed previously, many sales professionals are prone to not returning calls expediently. In other words, a consumer may call on Tuesday at 10 a.m. and not receive a return call until Thursday at 4 p.m. The number of telephone calls and appointments, the number of meetings, and the number of voicemails is unimportant to customer follow-up. When a customer calls a follow-up call must be returned within a convenient time. For example, I return all calls within 90 minutes. This may be impossible for some; however, it does show customer concern. Therefore, determine a short-term algorithm to return all customer calls. Yet do not believe that the call can be returned through e-mail or a simple text message. I know many of you reading this based upon age believe that your culture would agree with these communication methods. Untrue! Nothing is more important than the customer and if they've left you a voice message they expect one in return.

Last, avoid the easy way out. E-mails and text messages are not proper customer communication methods. This is especially true if your B2B sales transactions are in the hundreds of thousands if not millions. During my workshops, I'm often asked why I question the type of selling professionals carry with them. This is simply because customers judge individuals with the image they portray. So, a selling professional bringing a two-dollar pen to $100 million real estate transaction will be looked at indifferently. Therefore, any selling professional using e-mail for follow-up rather than a phone call will be viewed similarly. You must act the part.

Professionalism

With over 30 years of business experience, I have seen the best and worst of corporate professionalism. By this I mean when I first arrived at work all men wore suits and ties and women wore business suits. During the 1990s, Wall Street met some changes with something known as "dress-down Fridays." This allowed Wall Street traders, financial analysts, and portfolio managers to dress casually because the afternoon was dedicated to entertaining customers on the Hamptons and at several weekend events from Memorial Day through Labor Day. Unfortunately, in the late 1990s and then extending into the new millennium, this practice carried forth and became even more casual. Every day now seems to be a casual day. Research has indicated that it has lessened the productivity and even professionalism.

With this in mind, most industries today have a casual dress atmosphere. However, all selling professionals are the emulation of their company's character. They are the frontline to the customer, and they are the first person that any customer sees after the customer has conducted intense research. It is incumbent on every selling professional that they trust apart. What this means to you is that your shoes, your pants, your shirts, and your hairstyle must all emulate your company, your profession, and your industry. Further, you should have the appropriate tools of the trade; this includes but is not limited to a professional-looking padfolio, a professional briefcase, appropriate pens, and the elimination of excessive jewelry. And, in certain industries all tattoos are hidden from the customer. Selling professionals must present themselves in the best image possible at all times to the consumer. Anything less illustrates a lack of professionalism and focus on customer service.

Finally, since so many customers have access to research and information on the company's products, all selling professionals must be thorough. Today's selling professional should conduct as much research as possible on the customers' company, the industry, and its competitors. There are numerous tools that could be used such as Hoover's profiles, annual reports if the company is public, and the company's website. No selling professional should walk into a meeting unprepared. Today's customer wants somebody who could be consultative and provide value rather than just pitch a product.

Training

Selling professionals must also realize that foundational support has altered. Prior to the Great Recession of 2008, sales training in the United States and around the world was a multibillion-dollar industry. However, firms today are consumed by two thoughts: profits and productivity. Training eats into taking away both money and time. Therefore, selling professionals are not trained. Sellers simply must produce. The old "put up or shut up" mentality reigns supreme on both Main Street and Wall Street.

There is a twofold issue. First, the complexity of selling as outlined in this chapter is altered. Consumers have more information today, so the training of yesteryear will not work in today's complex sales process. Second, market turbulence does not allow sales professionals to be taken out of production. This impacts sales. Therefore to eliminate time and expense, selling professionals must develop their own training program. And, foundational selling will not do it. For example, when I first entered sales it was imperative to learn the art of negotiation, presentation, the sales process, and so on. These skills are no longer as imperative. Why, you might ask? Simply because today's selling professionals either have these unique innate traits or they don't.

Complex decision-making criteria are required. The new selling representative will think strategically not transactionally. In other words, consumers will make decisions based on the selling professional's desire to create a trusting relationship rather than sell a product. Sellers must understand the business, the business issues, the competition, and the industry and help the buyer to make more informed decisions. Therefore, the sellers will not have to deal with a subordinate because they will understand just as much about the business as the buyer and will enable him or her to make better decisions to remain competitive. To that end, sellers must acquire a voracious appetite for information. And, with today's technology this becomes easier. Yet, sellers will need to learn to read an annual report, understand financial statements, and develop the skills needed to understand competition.

Additionally, sellers will also need some development in questioning skills. Good sellers will need to understand the importance of listening to gain the insight required to scope, direct, and conclude useful discussion. Proper communication allows the seller to "listen" to hidden cues as well as better understand company issues. The acquisition of these skills helps to become a better strategic thinker and buyer peer.

Value

Finally, sellers under the new norm are required to sell based on value. You might ask, "What is value?" Value stems from two ideologies: (a) it is the benefit received from the buyer based on his or her assessment of the fee and (b) it is then the time, energy, and differentiation produced by the seller to the buyer. For the most part, many consumers due to the availability of information get tired of paying high prices without receiving value. Clearly, organizations such as Apple, Zappos, the Ritz Carlton, Disney to name a few place high regard for follow-up, service, results, accountability, and actions among other numerous ideals. Edward Jones, for example, establishes an outlet within the consumer's neighborhood so that the financial representative is constantly available. To the consumer, this is valuable. The seller is available to address questions, concerns, and suggestions and be within earshot of consumer needs. Consumers therefore are accepting of paying a higher fee to receive these services. In fact, research has always proven that all sales are emotional. Personal value is more than two times more likely to drive advocacy for a purchase than appeals to business value.

The availability factor is urgent in today's service-based economy. Most consumers make up their minds prior to actually saying "yes." During sales of commodities or even staple items (i.e., fuel, food, condiments, beverages), consumers are 75 percent ready to invoke a sale since their purchases are predetermined. However, when a consumer requires a seller to help make a decision, it is required of the seller to make it easier for customers to do business. A great seller in the new norm teaches customers how to purchase, what to consider, what to evaluate, and how to productively debate a purchase. This principle then defies commoditization by offering the value required for a consumer to ignore price and place his or her entire decision on value. We see this in industries such as real estate, high-end technology purchases, and complex B2B decisions. Such criteria employ a customer-centric model that defies price weighing all present and future decisions on relationship and value.

Consequently, the world of selling much like the world around us is undergoing chronic change. We are undergoing a revolution of new techniques, new ideologies, new communications, and new innovations. As such, remaining stagnant affects competition and erodes performance. Sellers and their managers who remain stagnant will lose business, consumers, and quite possibly their present roles. Innovation creates new opportunities. Even during failures, innovative strategies are developed to help improve human and business performance. Change is required to advance customer relationships, productivity, and profitability. The global environment continually changes.

Best Practices and Action Steps

- Begin to dress more appropriately. Buy clothes that create a business perspective and dressing better than the customer.
- Learn a new technology such as an app or software product that assists you with being more available to your clients.
- Return all customer calls in 90 minutes or less; learn to be more proactive and responsive to clients.
- Create a portfolio of business intelligence that allows you to offer consultative advice to your client. Learn to be a peer not just a vendor.
- Create testimonials, case studies, video reviews, and other media that illustrate results you provide to clients. Let your clients tell prospective clients of your value.
- Determine one item you can improve upon today and develop the skills to become a better selling professional.

A word before you change the page: This book is written so that you can develop singular ideas by reading one chapter at a time or just those chunks you believe most valuable. However, before you turn the page to address the next item, I want you to think about something. If you had one thing you can change as a selling professional what might it be? What might you do to become better? The reason I ask is that selling today is different than it was 10 to 15 years ago. It requires some harsh and subtle changes so that you can become more competitive and not only be at the top of your game—but your industry!

References

Adamson, B., M. Dixon, and N. Toman. July 1, 2012. "The End of Solution Sales." *Harvard Business Review*. http://hbr.org/2012/07/the-end-of-solution-sales/ar/1 (accessed February 5, 2014).

Brown, L., and C. Brown. 2014. "Diagnose Your Customer Culture." *Harvard Business Review*, January 17. (accessed January 13, 2016).

Crosby, T., and T. Stanton. January 22, 2014. "A Conference Call in Real Life." Tyler and Tripp Television. www.youtube.com/watch?v=DYu_bGbZiiQ

Peltea, A. 2014. "2014: The State of Worldwide Internet, Social Media and Mobile Penetration." Last modified January 10, 2014, http://adelinapeltea.com/2014-the-state-of-worldwide-internet-social-media-and-mobile-penetration/ (accessed February 5, 2014).

CHAPTER 2

The Cancellation of Old Practices

There are tremendous changes in consumer buying patterns, customer behaviors, and selling processes. Years ago, selling required onsite demonstrations and "live" representatives. Today, customer conversations are conducted over the Internet and demonstrations are arranged with apps and cloud computing. In fact, to a large extent, consumers have full access to vendor information and products. They self-educate due to lack of time and budgets.

Although there is a profound need for selling professionals, the increased use of technology has minimized numerous sales roles since the consumer has access to voluminous amounts of information. The customer is now in control, more so than ever before, requiring that sales professionals terminate aged practices in the hope that there is a focus on the customer. Customers do not want or need to be sold to. *In fact, they know more about your business, your industry, and your company than ever before.* If they want it, they will connect with you. Customers are smarter and more connected than ever. That said, *the key differentiator is the service, support, and systems you provide to engage clients*—it is all about the customer experience. To that end, transactional sales have ended, to be replaced by value and relationship.

The entire notion of customer experience is vital because most of the interactions between consumer and organization are service related. In fact, a simple research illustrates that 98 percent of U.S.-based organizations are service-oriented. Given that most of these firms hire selling representatives and also noting that interactions with consumers come in the form of direct, telephone, or e-mail, it is vital to ensure that the customer has a great experience at both the introduction and conclusion of every interaction. Do not be confused that this mention is solely customer service but rather an entire interaction between consumer and organization to glean the best value from the products and services provided. Customer service will be discussed in Chapter 4, but it is important to note this new evolution of customer interaction.

The customer wants a deeper involvement with the organization and its personnel. For too many years, consumers have jumped from company to company for the purposes of decreased cost and to a certain extent ease of negotiation. For example, we have seen many organizations and consumers cut ties with the cable television, telephone, and many other industries simply because of price and unsatisfactory service. Yet in today's world, time is money and both are lacking for the customer. Since the Great Recession of 2008, organizations are running short on time, profits, and productivity. To that end, many organizations today are seeking to build homogeneous relationships with organizations so that there is one point of contact, there is a higher level of understanding of the consumer's objectives, as well as helping the customer to competitively position itself within their industry. These qualities are tremendous asset to the consumer who is willing to pay handsomely. The implied value exponentially decreases time, stress, and research because the firm and its selling professionals acutely focus on the customer's specific needs. New evidence shows how a strong customer culture drives future business performance and supports numerous market strategies.

Case Study Example

For many years, the Ritz Carlton in Naples has provided exemplary customer experiences. Rather than worry about titles and responsibilities, any member of the team ensures that everything that touches the consumer is done personally, professionally, and passionately. The team spirit leads to increased bookings, lower attrition among staff, and a very high conference booking because of the clientele. In another example, The Chateau Elan Resort in Georgia offers "silver service without the gloves"—a customer experience set among vineyards, in a relaxing atmosphere where any request is answered with "consider it done" (Harvard Business Review 2014).

The expansion of customer centricity is a paradigm, in which sellers and managers must operate. The mission, vision, value, and passion must be centered on consumer experiences by lessening the resistance to perform a transaction versus entering a relationship. Transactions are conducted in retail and fast food establishments where consumers are price conscious, but in the world of business-to-business selling, consumers want value. And, this increased value will lead to higher future profits.

If centricity is important, what role does value play? The interesting thing is value is part of the customer-centric formula. There are various interpretations of the definition of value; for many, it could be price, perception of value, perception of just asking, or it might even be the return on the initial investment. After so many years of working with customers, the belief is that value is derived from the consumer's perception of the relationship, the quality of the service provided, and the fee in achieving the consumer's goals and purpose. Sometimes value is easily identifiable and sometimes it isn't.

There is intrinsic value, which is the value placed on a particular item or service. For example, a Timex's intrinsic value is approximately $200 while a standard Rolex is between $5 and $10,000. This value comes from the manufacturing or service provider who has conducted research to determine this value. Then there is perceived value, which is the value placed by the consumer based on their perception of the product/services' worth. The perception is based on the emotion, passion, and conviction consumers have with the product/service. Moreover, it is difficult to place a fee because each consumer places his or her worth based on his or her relationship and interest in the brand experience. For example, I tend to drink a lot of coffee because I enjoy it as well as enjoy conversations with friends over a cup of coffee. Coincidentally, I tend to like good deep roasted coffee and as such I frequently visit Starbucks. There are times I use carryout and other times where I engage in conversation. Yet, coffee at Starbucks is $2.50, and for me, it is worth every penny because the waiters know me by first name, brew my cup without asking, and frequently provide me free service. That is value four or five times more than the cup of coffee. To me, it is more than a commodity.

In order to understand customer value especially for the seller, it is important to be in customer's shoes. You should call the company and see what the interaction is between the front desk and attempting to reach a selling professional. There should be an understanding when calls are placed on hold or the selling professional is unavailable. Additionally, a seller should also understand the ordering process, logistics such as shipping and handling, as well as points in billing, billing issues, and even quality service issues. All selling professionals must understand what the customer gains or loses from conducting business with you. For example, Southwest Airlines at one time was known exponentially as a discount service and prided itself for it. Although Southwest heavily discounted its fares in order to sustain vital traffic, it also harped exponentially on customer value. Call and gate times were minimized to ensure that passengers were moving smoothly from all ports of call. Even the old CEO, Herb Kelleher, was known for loading bags on planes to ensure passenger movement. Because of the highly successful customer-centric service found on Southwest, it is noted that many passengers would pay two to three times more to enjoy such service on Southwest or any other air carrier!

For selling professionals and managers this is vitally important because there is much at stake to ensure the customer's satisfaction. Today's selling professional must comprehend that they are more than just representatives; they are organizational ambassadors employed to ensure successful client experiences. Therefore, sales attitude, experience, personality, behavior, and education are paramount toward achieving customer success. Ignorance of such qualities especially in today's competitive world will make it increasingly harder to achieve the productivity required from present executive management. This new level of experience and new level of service attempts to bring about a "new normalcy" to the world of selling requiring an alteration of habits from generations past.

Items That Require Immediate Changes

1. **Cold calling:** Dump it. It is very discouraging to see how many people believe this rote methodology still works. In the age of caller ID, the number of gatekeepers, and simply busyness, people are too

busy. Cold calling is a disruption. It wastes time. Very few are successful at it, and very little product is sold. Money is better spent
increasing visibility and representatives investing in customer-centric
relationships.

2. **Customer response:** Return calls when promised. Customers do
   not appreciate being placed on indefinite hold. Customers desire
   immediate conversations with those who can offer assistance. Not
   returning calls or hiding behind voice mail is an excuse for a customer
   to discover your competitor.

3. **Customer service:** There is research that illustrates that over
   50 percent of customer interaction is service related. Treat your
   customers correctly by becoming engaged. Be in the moment.
   Become genuinely interested in their concerns. Have representatives
   smile and be interested in engaging with the customer. Certainly,
   sales people have bad days, but the client does not need to know and
   does not care. Service must be paramount. Selling departments must
   also build a service-oriented culture.

4. **Selling versus building relationships:** Social networking groups
   are besieged with conversation about "selling to the c–suite." Not
   only is it interesting to discover so many self-proclaimed experts, but
   more ironic to view the opinions on how to sell to senior executives.
   Herein is the best advice. *Senior Executives do not want to be sold
   anything.* They desire healthy conversations that build relationships
   with trusted peers. Senior officers know what they need and when
   they need it. Representatives must be keener to the issues of decision
   makers so that their conversations and questions allow them to be a
   peer of the buyer. Vendor thinking must end so that representatives
   focus on objectives, measurements of success, and value returned to
   the organization.

5. **Customer to Customer:** With the high levels of connectivity,
   customers are more interested today in hearing from other customers.
   People buy from those they know and trust. Individuals desire
   customer-centered relationships. Build your community with case
   studies, testimonials, and audio/video snippets that illustrate results
   from other customers. Sales departments want to ensure that their

customers become selling avatars. Good peer relationship clients provide relentless referrals for the business.

6. **Customer communication:** Technology is not the answer to everything. You must be constantly top of mind to avoid activities that diminish relationships. Stop the use of e-mail to communicate with clients. Pick up a telephone or send a simple handwritten thank you card. Illustrate your value, not the need to make commission.

7. **Customer discretion:** Customers are no longer in a hurry. Credit concerns, economic volatility, and shareholder return are more important than ever. In addition, the use of the Internet provides customers the necessary time to conduct the proper research before making decisions. A recent client researched John's firm for over six months. They conducted research and sought council from former clients and then signed a six-figure order. If you're client, they will come.

New Roles for Sales Managers and Selling Professionals

One of the largest issues for any sales manager is having the right personnel to do the job. For so many years, many sales managers simply hired individuals with either the "right personality" or the "proper raw skills" to sell. The fact is that selling, much like any other job, is a profession. Sales managers and their staff must treat it as such. Though many organizations advertise "no experience necessary" when posting new sales positions, a growing number of organizations have begun focusing on recruiting actual sales professionals. Sales managers need to first and foremost seek the proper talent. In the words of Jim Collins taken from his national bestselling book, *Good to Great*, you must "have the right people on the bus." No longer can selling managers simply hire "great guys" to sell, they must hire professionals who understand the complexity of business, the need to build and foster relationships, and the desire to understand the customers' needs and industry in a consultative manner. Sales managers need to hire those nonconventional individuals who have a desire to build relationships, create a presence, understand strategy, and bring the customer results. So, what is required here?

First, the methods as depicted in Chapter 1 must end. The days of cold calling, door knocking, and cutting names out from newspapers and magazines are over! I know of one public seminar company that even in 2014 used the notion of "55 calls per day" as a means to drum up training and consulting business. This is not selling; it is bullying representatives. The company is bullying its representatives to make calls and they in turn bully customers into making decisions quickly. This useless and tasteless motive must end. Cold calling is dead as are many of the practices developed in the pre-Internet and electronic days. Therefore, sales managers must constantly seek agents who have the raw talents that can build relationships. Selling is just that—a relationship business—and those who develop this concept do well; those who don't, fail miserably.

There are several nuances to the idea of relationship, and it begins with both the selling professional and the sales manager. Finding the right talent denotes that representatives become a peer of the buyer and not just an order taker. Sales managers therefore must hire individuals who are fearless of titles, narcissism, and identity. And, they need to hire those who never suffer the triviality of being subordinated. In other words, the sales professional hired must be strong enough in personality to acknowledge that he or she is a peer of the buyer, desirous of identifying problem areas for the client, and helping to achieve results. This level of selling professional will produce more results for the sales organization, alleviate management issues for the sales manager, and achieve better service for the client. Therefore, taking the time to hire such a person is more desirous then hiring "just anyone."

Second, in helping to build relationships, sales managers must hire individuals who take heed to the idea of presence. Let's face it; we are all creatures of habit and selling professionals are no different. From the ancient times until approximately the 1990s, selling professionals achieved zero leads in many instances by being reactive. However, sales managers must hire individuals who are much more proactive. Yet, being proactive is not just a matter of networking, it is a matter of building both an online and on-the-ground presence. Selling professionals today must become more adept at networking with their customer. They must find the key decision-maker and determine places and organizations they visit so that the selling professional can network with them. Additionally, selling professionals must engage in online activity that allows them to network with individuals for the purposes of achieving relationships. This means that selling professionals must engage in blogs, search engine optimization, Internet strategies, and social media strategies so that they can influence relationships 24 hours per day, seven days per week. When someone is in need of a solution that needs to be resolved, the selling professional who illustrates a valuable online presence while also achieving a decent reputation can typically be the key differentiator that a prospective party seeks. Selling professionals who enlist good reputation management are no different than organizational sites such as yelp.com, health grades.com, or any of the other online sites that organizations use for reputation management.

Third, sales managers must hire people who build value. Value is no different in the sales world than it is in the marketing world. In fact, selling is part of the entire marketing process. To that end, I mean that prospective individuals will purchase for value. This is the benefit and results achieved by the potential client that they want or need. In order to capture prospective individuals who are seeking value, the selling professional today cannot just sit back and wait for the phone to ring or e-mail to come across his or her screen. Today's selling professional must constantly be building a community that understands the value they bring to the market; this is what will attract the community to the selling profession. There are several methods to help develop this value, here are just a few:

> **Referrals:** Proper networking and sales etiquette involve referral acquisition. Similar to gaining closure agreement, many professionals abhor asking for the order! Business is driven by the ability to ask for new business. If clients are happy with your work, they will gladly and willingly provide you with referrals. The best time to seek referrals is when you are first engaged with the client and they are in that emotional high. More importantly, you want to ask when you are in the account, since this is the best time to be top of mind.
>
> Another imperative item to remember is that there is strength in numbers. The more referrals you obtain, the fuller the pipeline.

There is a story of an insurance professional who would visit clients and not leave without three new referrals. Even if the client provided one or two, the agent would not leave until he received three or more. Remember this is the easiest part of the lead-generation process—ask for your referrals.

Follow-up on referrals: It might seem pragmatic, yet there is much evidence to illustrate that many professionals do not follow up. Friends, family, and current clients typically provide these golden nuggets so it is vital that follow-up occurs. A rule of thumb is 24 hours from receipt to contact.

Speaking: The number one fear is public speaking. Aside from cold calling, it is the second most relevant way to obtain leads. Every business professional is an expert in his or her market and has something to share. Speaking is an opportunity to meet new individuals while allowing the leads to come to you.

Developing brand: The laws of persuasion and attraction operate efficiently when the organization or its employees are branded. Individuals become persuaded by name recognition, whether an individual in an organization or the firm itself. Building your personal brand is a terrific method to create sales attraction. Do you have a sentence, a tagline, or a name that can create a personal brand?

Teaching: During the draft of this book, a former student approached me, "Do you have February 23rd available, I need to book you for a keynote!" That is leverage. I am an adjunct professor at universities because I love teaching, and it also helps to establish a sales funnel. Teaching is a wonderful approach to community service and a great method to generate leads. Do you have expertise in an area that can be shared with others?

Fourth, one of the biggest differences about today's selling professional that most sales managers need to understand is that today's professional is no longer the order taker, but an authority. Selling professionals today must create a platform that allows key decision-makers and even influencers to view their expertise. Sales managers must allow their professionals to share their expertise that encourages reputation building. Some of the key factors that allow professionals to share this authority are: speaking at industry events and writing articles in regional and national publications. There are certain organizations that will require certain levels of monitoring such as the insurance or stock brokerage community because of Securities and Exchange Commission regulations. However, those individuals who create a platform instantly engage others with solutions for a myriad of today's issues. Other methods of sharing authority and expertise include, but are not limited to, speaking at webinars, national conventions, and industry-related tradeshows. When one becomes an authority in his or her vertical market, he or she will do so before the competitor is even aware that they exist. This will create an incredible differentiated advantage while making the sales professionals an extremely valuable resource to their organization.

Best Practice and Action Steps

Selling today is very different, and it requires today's professionals to make the needed changes to be competitive and successful. There are many things you might do to help become better, but here are just a few of the intangible suggestions to make you improve greatly over a 30- to 60-day period.

- Use voice mail, e-mail, and text messages as an appropriate means to remain in contact with your clients. The key requirement today is communication. The more you communicate with your clients the better return on investment.
- Learn to create your value proposition or unique selling proposition. This is a very succinct statement that illustrates how you assist your prospective clients head and shoulders above the competition. Rather than just say that you're selling professional, you might want to suggest that you transform struggling information-technology departments into successful resource partners.
- Stop utilizing old technology such as cold calling and knocking on doors. If you really want to be successful in the

sales game then you really need to understand how to build a collection of referrals that gets you in the door easier.

- Learn more about your customer. Conduct intense information gathering so that you become a buyer here and not necessarily a vendor. The more you understand your client, the better off you will be in illustrating that you're not just another vendor.
- One of the items that will be discussed in Chapter 8 but you can begin doing here is to learn how to get to the key decision-maker. Stop being subordinated on sales calls, successful people only deal with decision-makers.
- Use handwritten business cards. Take a moment to put down your personal cell number or personal home number. Additionally, utilize handwritten thank you cards to provide your value and personalization toward customer service.
- Develop a list of key provocative questions that must be asked during every sales interaction. Stop utilizing some of the commonplace questions that are tired and aged. Developing a list of questions based upon the client's objectives measurements for success, and values will help you create a better relationship with interested parties.
- Invest 20 to 30 minutes every day to learn something new about your client, the industry, or even the sales profession. The best individuals I like are athletes in the field; they are always conditioning to become more fit.

Just a quick word before you move to the next chapter; I've already mentioned that this book is set up to help you eliminate many of your old sales habits. Some of those habits include cold calling, utilizing items such as the Yellow Pages, and making calls without a deep understanding of the people that you're calling. Some of these tactics were used in the early days of the profession, but due to our contemporary society they are no longer useful. In the next chapter, I'm going to help you understand how to eliminate some of those old practices and make you more successful in utilizing technologies that work. That means that you're going to have to make some changes, become uncomfortable, escape from your comfort zone, and create new habits. Yet, at the end of the day, you will be better off for it because you'll be more successful than anyone in your industry, your company, and perhaps even the profession!

CHAPTER 3

New Methods for Selling

To help establish a sense of this chapter, it is going to be useful to understand that the age-old technologies no longer work. There are too many organizations today that have higher selling professionals to make cold calls. Many of these organizations provide new selling professionals very large lists of names and telephone numbers, and tell them that they must make 150 calls before the end of the day. These tactics do not work! Today's consumer is much smarter, and they lack the time and patience. Therefore, selling professionals should be better at getting in front of the prospective client so that they can meet their sales goals and earn commission. By deeply understanding consumer buying patterns and by dropping processes that create obstacles, today's selling professional will be better than the sales game.

According to CSO Insights, "Sales Performance Optimization 2009 Survey Results and Analysis," an astonishing 54 percent of 1,800 firms fail to turn leads into a meeting more than half of the time. For any small business owner, this is the primary stumbling block. If your sales team cannot get you in through the door of a prospective client, how can your company survive? Effective lead generation is your most powerful component to increasing sales productivity.

The current rules of business have changed significantly as a result of constantly updated technology and the relentless strain on time management. Organizations must become more nimble to the needs of clients and much more efficient with selling effectiveness. Too much labor is involved with issues other than producing leads. Too little time is spent with economic buyers and establishing value-based relationships. The hub of selling effectiveness requires lead generation, not only getting them into the pipeline, but through it! Figure 3.1 illustrates the variety of concepts used to show how leads are to come into the pipeline and eventually flow out to become a true lead that may provide a sale.

Attracting leads as a web attracts bugs

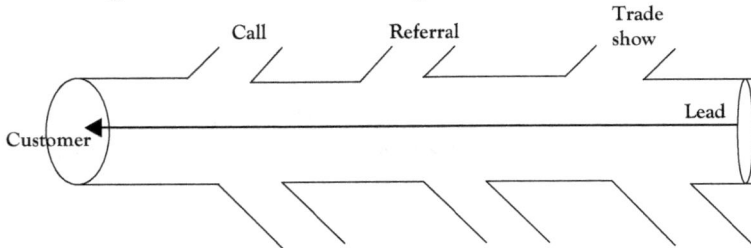

Figure 3.1 The pipeline

There are three lead-generation strategies:

- Prospecting opportunities
- Value-based selling
- Process selling

Prospecting Opportunities—Is There Gold in Those Names?

Contacts for business are similar to gold bullion in a stream. Consumer buying processes are altered with the proliferation of technology and global communication. Clients now know more information about the company and basics prior to the first contact.

The requirement is that businesses and their peers get into the sales game sooner. The longer it takes to establish contact, the larger the gap and easier for clients to find competitors. Value must be presented quickly or otherwise conversations are lost.

Cold calling, direct mail, and other traditional selling methods do little to build relationships. When was the last time you took a call in the evening after a lengthy day from a cold calling manic? When conducting workshops and consulting, I advocate that before selling professionals pick up the telephone and state "Hello," they must have information on whom they are calling. Sales intelligence requires the use of industry information and proper research to understand information on the company, its chief competitors, and the industry. A review of current customers and issues affecting the company are useful since the content can be used to drive discussion with the economic buyer. Another interesting perspective is that sellers are outsiders, and they see trends and threats that customers might not.

The most bountiful sources of company information come directly from annual reports, national newspapers, and even the Internet. A simple Google search helps those searching for client information with a wealth of content. There are databases such as Sorkins and Leadership Directories that offer content-rich profiles.[1] The information on company, competition, and products/services is used to drive discussion.

Not All People Are Created Equal

Another helpful lead-generation technique is targeting and segmenting your markets. These need to be done with utmost thought and rigor. Target market selection is an imperative tactic of selling. You need to know who your best potential clients are.

Targeting assists in dissecting the total population of potential clients into a microcosm of those most possible to speak with. Similar to the manner of moving leads through the pipeline, target market selection creates a subset of possibilities. There are four methods to dividing the market:

1. **Geographic segmentation:** Location specific. Lead generation is produced by choosing a location within 100 miles of the corporation's headquarters; thus enabling better customer service and customer interaction.
2. **Demographic segmentation:** Measurable statistics include, but are not limited to, age, race, sex, religion, ethnicity, income, and so on. Conversations related to products and services are aided with better comprehension of client's values and perspective.
3. **Psychographic segmentation:** Lifestyle preferences and their attitudes, interests, and desires. As buyers detail preferences, the conversations immediately relate to value. Competitive differentiation is vital here.

---

[1] I make no compensation from these. There are other similar databases, which are also used as examples. Many of these points may already be familiar.

4. **Behavioristic segmentation:** Values and beliefs, and desired benefits. Conversations are stimulated by focusing on the benefits that relate to customer needs.

In addition to the aforesaid strategies, here are some tactical elements to assist in lead generation.

Low-Hanging Fruit

We know so many individuals, yet we do not tap into the vital resources that can help us. Sometimes seeking business opportunities is as simple as calling a friend or removal from the comfort zone to walk over to your neighbor's home. Business requires chutzpah! You have two choices: (1) You can sit behind a desk pondering how to get business or (2) Step up in front of someone's desk requesting it!

Networking

The best professionals constantly network. Good professionals by nature require constant engagement with others to comprehend business trends and meet new opportunities. For over 27 years, I have attended at least one or two networking events per month, and I can attribute a number of leads and new clients to this practice. Admittedly, there exist a plethora of networking associations and organizations. Choose those close to your location and aligned with your business. How can anyone know your business with just a shingle hanging in the breeze?

Referrals

Proper networking and sales etiquette involve referral acquisition. Similar to gaining closure agreement, many professionals abhor asking for the order! Business is driven by the ability to ask for new business. If clients are happy with your work, they will gladly and willingly provide you with referrals. The best time to seek referrals is when you are first engaged with the client and they are in that emotional high. More importantly, you want to ask when you are in the account, since this is the best time to be top of mind.

Another imperative item to remember is that there is strength in numbers. The more referrals you obtain, the fuller the pipeline. There is a story of an insurance professional who would visit clients and not leave without three new referrals. Even if the client provided one or two, the agent would not leave until he received three or more. Remember this is the easiest part of the lead-generation process—ask for your referrals.

Follow-up on Referrals

It might seem pragmatic, yet there is much evidence to illustrate that many professionals do not follow up. Friends, family, and current clients typically provide these golden nuggets so it is vital that follow-up occur. A rule of thumb is 24 hours from receipt to contact.

There are many valuable activities for small business owners to improve lead generation. How many are you engaged in now?

Speaking

The number one fear is public speaking. Aside from cold calling, it is the second most relevant way to obtain leads. Every business professional is an expert in his or her market and has something to share. Speaking is an opportunity to meet new individuals while allowing the leads to come to you.

Developing Brand

The laws of persuasion and attraction operate efficiently when the organization or its employees are branded. Individuals become persuaded by name recognition, whether an individual in an organization or the firm itself. Building your personal brand is a terrific method to create sales attraction. Do you have a sentence, a tagline, or a name that can create a personal brand?

Teaching

During the draft of this book, a former student approached me, "Do you have February 23rd available, I need to book you for a keynote!" That is leverage. I am an adjunct professor at universities because I love teaching, and it also helps to establish a sales funnel. Teaching is a wonderful approach to community service and a great method to generate leads. Do you have expertise in an area that can be shared with others?

Value-Based Selling

The way to avoid the trap of being just a regular selling professional and a high achiever is to refrain from the traditional model of features and benefits. Look at the client in terms of outcomes and results. No matter what the issue is, focus on how your organization provides the results the client seeks. It is not about facts, but the return on the client's investment.

Building your business is not about making money, but about creating relationships and clients. The conversation with prospects should not be about features, but rather the value from you and your product/service. Do not focus on fees, commissions, costs, or any other sales-related words. If the discussion is not about value then you have surrendered control of the discussion, and the result will not be in your preferred terms. I recall a great quote from a mentor, Alan Weiss Seminar,

"Language controls discussion, discussion controls the relationship, and relationship controls the business."

When the conversation focuses on value, the prospect becomes convinced of the knowledge you provide and desires a relationship with you. Therefore, all discussions must focus on how working with your organization produces returns for the client with minimal investment in time and money.

Methods to Illustrate Value

Discover Objectives

Ask the client to provide three objectives they desire with the use of your services. People act on emotion; therefore, if your questions concentrate on needed objectives, especially if they apply to need, then you will create value. Prudent questions focus on future vision, future outcome, and future efficiencies. Clients today seek two things: profits and productivity. When your questions focus on client objectives, they indicate aspirations for business improvement.

Sample Questions for Objectives and Value

- Ideally, what would you like to accomplish?
- What is the ideal outcome that you want to establish?
- How will you know we've accomplished the objective?
- What does this mean to you personally?
- How will this affect performance?
- What is the intangible impact?

Additional Outcomes

In my entire business career, so many automatically know what they want, but few know what they need. Ask additional questions that provide value by honing in on these differences. The focus here is on value to the organization and to the individual, as well as measurements for success.

Focus on Output, Not Input

No one cares about your creative advertising or corporate office. Demonstrate important outcomes for the client, such as speed, guarantees, high return, and transition management. When you focus on client results, conversations become crisp and tightly focused.

Listen

I recall buying a car many years ago. I was not focused on price, but rather on features. Yet most of the salespeople insisted on delivering a pitch, telling me how to drive, or suggesting features that did not interest me. You cannot learn while you are talking. Develop provocative questions and keep the prospect talking until you have enough emotional and factual information to embrace them as partners. When you listen, and clients talk, you also obtain better information.

Buyer

Question
path

Seller

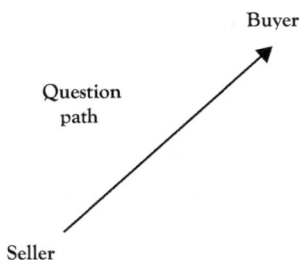

Figure 3.2 Asking the right questions

Testimonials

People like to conduct business with those whom they know and like. Begin by obtaining a testimonial from every possible client. Relationships are built based on prior expertise. Your ability to nimbly build a "book" of testimonials will assist you in becoming the provider of choice.

Decision Makers

Gatekeepers waste time and do not understand value. Gatekeepers focus on victimhood and conceit. Decision makers concern themselves with productivity and value. Do not be confused by titles. There are many individuals who believe titles have enormous clout. Sixty-seven percent of business professionals spend too much time with those who cannot make a decision. Sellers are often duped into the process because they do not ask the proper questions. Good detective work means asking the difficult questions.

Process Selling—Selling Is a Process, Not an Event

Clients purchase from people they like and trust. That statement is so compelling that I need to repeat it once again so that you fully understand its importance: *clients purchase from people they like and trust*. It is quite possible that they do not trust you. People want honest information about what the service can do for them. This fundamental issue is the key to selling success. Ethics are difficult to instruct—you have them or you don't!

Here are the most important rules about selling that I have learned over the years:

1. There are four simple steps (as described ahead) of selling that are vital. You do not need numerous methods and training. Learn the four simple steps and you will sell more than you realize.
2. There is no basic selling rule or principle that has been discovered in the last 100 years.
3. You need to take these principles and use them daily. Practicing these rules and making them a habit in your daily life will make you better.
4. Do not rush learning. Rome was not built in a day. You must learn daily and practice daily but without haste and impatience.
5. Evaluate yourself. Be critical and learn by what you are doing and not doing to become better. Be honest in your assessment.

In order to achieve, you must be client and you must have faith to become better each day.

Selling is not an overnight process. Selling is a profession that takes years to master, and even then, there is always something to learn. There is no way that in three weeks you will become proficient in selling. Nor can it occur in one sales training course. Selling, like human development, is a process that will take you years of time, energy, and investment. Similar to a stock, invest in yourself, and watch the returns soar to great heights.

Four primary steps in the selling process are as follows:

1. Prepare to present
2. Uncover the needs
3. Manage rapport and objections
4. Provide closure

I have not only used these steps but also instructed for well over 27 years. I have trained over 60,000 selling professionals and have helped them achieve over a half billion dollars in gross revenues. These steps have worked for them, and they will work for you too!

This is what you need to know:

1. The prospect might be interested and you might have their attention, but your inability to build a relationship impacts moving forward. To that end, prospects will object to your offer. You must understand how to move forward to create further interest so that they trust you!

2. Unless you are asking provocative questions and illustrating concern for the prospect, they will go elsewhere. Uncovering needs means asking the difficult questions to understand those needs.

3. It is vital to keep your prospect's attention so that they remain interested. If prospects are interested in your offer and they "hear" the benefits, they are more likely to listen and invest the time with your offer.

4. The most fascinating yet most daunting part of any sale is closure. Procrastination and indecision are a part of life. Moreover, many professionals are afraid to ask for the business. The best way to make money and get more clients is to ask.

P-R-A-C-T-I-C-E Selling—Your GPS to Selling

Ninety-two percent of all sales professionals do not use or have a formal selling process. This ultimately affects pipeline movement and closure ratio. Einstein once stated, "Insanity is doing the same thing continually and expecting a different result." My experience in the field and working particularly with athletes has helped me develop the process I want to introduce to you. My belief is that athletes *practice* to obtain strengths in performance; attorneys *practice* to become more efficient with litigation or servicing clients; physicians *practice* since the body mechanics and issues differ from person to person; and musicians *practice* to better harmonize. Selling is a profession that requires continuous improvement in skills and relationships as well. As consumer behavior changes, sellers need to be more efficient with handling relationships and expectations. The only method to encourage them is to P-R-A-C-T-I-C-E.

A Breakdown of the P-R-A-C-T-I-C-E Method

Planning

The most vital process for any successful professional is planning. Planning is about information gathering and research. An acronym for plan is **P**lan to **Live And Never** be unhappy. Professionals must plan each call, and they must be prepared to offer information. Additionally, professionals must identify with research information to resolve the client's pains.

Rapport

Building rapport is one of the largest hurdles for any business professional. You have to get to know people, even strangers. This will challenge you daily. However, you must always be smiling and discover new ways to constantly influence people to resolve their issues.

Attention

Buyers today are much more distracted by e-mail, voice mail, snail mail, Internet, remote controls, cell phones, and so on. Professionals must rise above the static to be heard. And, more importantly, you must keep their attention so they are not distracted from you. Differentiation is your key to maintain attention.

Conviction

These are the tools that you need to convince your client to buy from you. Professionals typically carry an arsenal of information for sales calls. However, each call must be customized with the tools and techniques so that the buyer will "hear." Items such as testimonials, statistical studies, charts, graphs, and schematics are just some of the items you will need.

Time Management

It is imperative to work with efficiency. Good organizational and time management skills ensure your productivity and profitability.

Interest

If you want someone to buy something from you, it is imperative that you interest them. This means using tools and fact-finding techniques to determine if there is an alignment between you and the prospect.

And it requires the use of benefits to obtain the sale. Remember the rule—*prospects buy benefits.*

Close

Never forget to ask for the sale—what do you want to obtain. Closing is one of the most vital steps in the business process. If you do not close, you do not make any money. Remember when you close, use the ABC rule; *Always be closing!*

Evaluation and Education

Be enthusiastic about your product or service. You want to love what you do and you want to love what you sell. Your interest or lack of it will be revealed through every presentation. Even though rejection rears its ugly head in the sales game, your enthusiasm must remain unyielding.

Finally, enlightenment comes with each and every call. Learn something new with every sales call and each presentation. *Business professionals must be adept at lifelong learning!*

Best practices in action steps are:

- Selling is not process, it's an event. You must begin to create some strategies that are going to make you more successful.
- You need to operate similar to the way the worker operates—building relationships. You must become a relationship expert.
- Becoming a relationship expert requires you to do certain things that you've not done before, such as seeking out multiple referrals in the day, networking in a variety of associations, speaking about regional and national events, and quite possibly writing articles for local periodicals. Conducting this step will make you a media icon and attract people to you rather than the reverse.
- Take your resume to a local community college or private university and see if there's an opportunity to teach in the business department in marketing and management.

This will place you in front of numerous people who could quite possibly become your clients.

- Develop a list of provocative questions based upon objectives that the client would like to meet. Stop worrying about features and benefits of your product or service and begin to operate under the notion that the client is at the center of every interaction.

Just a quick word before you turn the next page. Have you ever been wowed by the interaction between you and us as professionals? Or, have you ever been completely turned off by someone who was supposed to help you at either a retail establishment or service organization? If you answered yes to both questions, you'll understand the importance of customer service. One of the items that sets any professional apart from others in the field is the relationship that he/she has with clients. Superb customer service allows people to talk about you in a variety of ways so that others understand why they should conduct business with you or your organization. Avatars in the field are Disney, Federal Express, and Nordstrom. Each has conducted a vast amount of customer service, allowing customers to flock to them without the need for advertisements, cold calling, or even commercials. Imagine coming into the office each and every day of your life with the phone ringing off the hook from people most interested in doing business with you! Imagine the reduction of labor you would have simply because of your great customer service agent. My advice when you turn the page is to think about those things you can do to create great customer service so that the phone rings off the hook and people say, "is this_____? I was told I need to order from you!"

CHAPTER 4

Creating a Customer Experience

There is an obvious implication in your reading this book from chapter to chapter. You will note that I'm creating emphasis on relationships and customer interaction. That is because in years past, the structure of most organizations was concerned with the "what's in it for me," approach. However, today's customer is concerned with the "what's in it for me" approach and those that make the transition from organization to customer focus will be more successful. There are several reasons for this. First, every organization has got to be concerned about the number one asset—the customer. It is the customer that decides what products and services are to be sold by the selling professional. Selfish selling professionals will not sell anything if customer service is poor. Second, and perhaps most important, with the use of technology customers speak to each other. Technology today especially with the use of social media will impact marketing and future sales if your customer service lacks—customers can speak badly about you. You have to develop the notion that one poor customer service report will appear on Facebook, Twitter, Instagram, Snapshot, YouTube, Vimeo, and many other social media platforms. Providing good customer service is a proper thing to do. The more customer representatives act as advocates from the initial conversation, the more potential clients you will attract, the more you will convert and the more you'll keep.

In contemporary world, we are witnessing increasing symbiotic relationship between the world of customer service and sales professionals. Customers are realizing that those representatives who pay heed to customer service are more successful individually, while also bringing more revenue into the organization. Additionally, organizations find that when customer service is superb, their advertising costs decrease. This is because great customer service helps to develop avatars who continually speak well about your company. When others speak well about you, they will tell the world. This loyalty will create not only a terrific base who continually returns to buy, but tells others about it too.

What is required today in most organizations is the vital need for customer service. You have probably heard that there is much banter about the focus for items such as customer satisfaction, customer service, customer loyalty, and even customer centricity. Yet, these are simply words on a piece of paper or in a television advertisement unless someone does something about it: the reason being that at the end of the day marketing and sales are all about relationships.

One of the biggest aspects about customer relationship management is simply the ideology of creating consumers who can become brand loyalists simply due to their passion for the intimate relationships they have with organizations. For example, how many great stories have been heard on the Internet, the news, or in social media dialogues about organizations such as Starbucks, Zappos, or the Ritz Carlton? None of these companies would exist without great customer centricity. It is because the organizations have become so immersed with teaching selling professionals the value of customers that each of these organizations has customers that are brand loyalists as well as evangelists. This is exactly what selling professionals need to do; they need to become ambassadors or brokers so that customers become so overwhelmingly desirous of not only products and services, but how they are treated.

Here are some simple facts to explain why the customer experience is so important. Poor customer experiences result in an estimated $83 billion loss by U.S. enterprises each year because of defections and abandoned purchases (*source*: Parature Customer Service Blog) and 89 percent of consumers began doing business with a competitor following a poor customer experience (*source*: RightNow Customer Experience Impact Report 2011). That's a huge statistic!

There are also several other pragmatic reasons why organizations desire to have better relationships with their consumers: (a) customers talk to other customers, thereby decreasing marketing costs and creating more buzz and (b) because of the fact that so many people utilize e-mail and other forms of electronic exchange such as social media, one keystroke can either increase or quickly decrease business. Therefore, it is extremely important today to ensure the fact that the customers are happy. Good talk will help us, and bad talk will kill us.

Customers provide the focus for the organization. Customers provide your company's success or failure. Customers can make or break an organization. The reason is if they are unhappy they will tell others and then they will leave your company to a competitor.

The key is to listen to the customer to ensure the organization's offering meets the customer's requirements. You need to think in terms of the customer. Here is an example using an acronym:

C = Have concern for the asset
U = Always attempt to discover their unique needs and expectations
S = Set expectations with customer
T = Treat them equally and with pride
O = Orient yourself and your team to customer outcomes
M = Make getting and keeping customers the goal
E = Engage the customer in relationship
R = Remember to evaluate all conversations to become better

In the following pages of this book, my plan is to describe for you several ideas to assist selling professionals, sales managers, and even small organizations without selling professionals how to get into the mind of the customer so that they can service them better, build better relationships, and gain the perspective of brand loyalists.

Get into the Mind-Set of Your Customers—What Do Customers Really Expect?

Customers today are much smarter than we think. Consumers today are most specifically concerned about value and trust. With many parties to choose from and access to websites, it is hard to distinguish one vendor from another. The key differentiator today is customer service.

Consumers want to ensure that they are treated right from the moment that they are serviced. This requires that organizations develop a customer culture. This means that everyone from the front desk to the executive suite cater to the needs of the customer. In fact, what customers really expect is that they are treated as the purpose of business and not an interruption to it.

When working with customers, there are four very specific things to be considered to help your organization become more customer service savvy. These include people, support, trust, and finally relationship.

People—The people you hire must provide a satisfactory service to the customer. This means smiling upon entry and even engaging the customer with great conversation that illustrates a peer relationship. Getting to know them and becoming genuinely interested in their business is very helpful to building good relationships. Examples here include Zappos and Southwest Airlines. Zappos, for instance, will have a conversation with customers and not be too concerned with others on hold. At that moment in time, you are the most important. In fact, their longest customer service call is six hours! Make certain your team does not rush callers off the phone but takes quality time to build relationships.

Support—When they call to get service, customers expect a real person to answer the phone. They don't expect to be placed on indefinite hold where circulating maze of voice operated options. Customers become very angry by the number of prompts they must provide in order to get the assistance needed. How many times do you call some companies and get press "one" for English, "two" for another language, then press "one" for sales, "two" for service, now enter your account number, then hit "three" if you know your child's first name. Many utility companies use these systems, but they are lengthy, confusing, too annoying, and most importantly not service savvy. I suggest that you have either live people answer the phone to make the customer feel more welcome or if you have to have a calling tree, make it friendlier with either less prompts, less repetition, or easier ways to reach a live person. And if you do use a tree, call it and see if you can discriminate it like a customer and implement changes you feel would make it easier.

Trust—The customer wants to know how you can help them as a trusted advisor. Customers are seeking solutions to problems, and there is expectancy that you could offer help based on previous experience. Give easier advice or help people find things on websites to help build the trust factor.

Relationship—Customers want to be treated as part of the business not as a barrier of entry. This includes being a part of product announcements, new product enhancements, repairs and maintenance, and perhaps even insight into new products. As an example, Procter & Gamble, the large consumer products company, operates several websites, focus groups, and even live laboratories that allow customers to provide feedback for new products and services. Such feedback has provided for new developments such as the Tide and Clorox sticks. You can also use new methods such as Facebook and Twitter to build relationships like some hospitals that use Twitter for emergency wait times and Facebook page for coupon announcements.

When you make your customers a part of the business and create partnerships, there is a better relationship and more trust. As the trust builds, they tell others of your honesty, helping to create more business for you and less attrition in the customer ranks. Customers want to stay with you; you just need to show them a bit more love!

What I'm going to do to assist you as a selling professional is divide certain areas of customer service into very detailed pragmatic sections with some action steps in each of the sections so that you understand the importance of customer service in each and you can make subtle changes so that you become a highly skilled and successful customer service agent in your competitive industry.

Discover What Customer Service Excellence Really Means—To You and To Your Customers

When was the last time that you were "Wowed"? When was the last time that you attended an event, visited a restaurant, or were serviced by someone where you were absolutely blown away? When we talk about the customer service experience, we really mean a consistent and relentless pursuit of ongoing customer service. You know when you arrive, and it is customer service no matter the time, the location, or the personnel. It seems to run rampant in the company. For example, when you visit certain restaurants, hotels, or department stores and the staff is always welcoming, friendly, and cannot wait to help.

Every single contact your organization has with its customers either cultivates or corrodes your relationship. That includes every letter you send, every ad you run, and every phone call you make. This includes contact from the first person to the senior officer. And by the way, since customer service is an internal function, this means that interdepartmentally people must service each other.

If you think about it, your business is only as good as your worst employee. When you think of how poorly you treat your employees, this actually becomes a domino effect to your overall asset—your customers. This is sobering simply because customer service is as much an internal function as it is externally. Imagine entering a store and hearing the screaming or sarcasm among two or more employees—or you hear employees speak poorly about a former customer. Would you return?

For example, I recently refinanced the mortgage on my home. There was an issue with some paperwork while finalizing the title. A woman named Holly helped me for the better part of five weeks in researching the information and actually placing phone calls for me so that the title would close in a timely manner. Holly lessened my labor by conducting research and making the calls for me, which is something that is not normally done by title companies. She was so client and so professional that I actually wrote a letter of commendation to her supervisor. She and her boss where interested in one thing—getting me the loan and making me happy.

Have you really walked through your own customer service strategy? What does it look like at the other end? Can you see yourself as your own client? Your only tools to ensure that customers are treated properly are to either (a) "mystery shop" the business so that you see whether customers are treated by your employees the way that you want them to be treated and (b) to empower your employees to make decisions so that they can execute in a timely fashion.

What is mystery shopping? If you are not familiar with this, all one needs for it is arrange for a "stranger" to shop your establishment the way a customer would. Have them call in or visit and take notes of all they experience.

Empowerment—Simply put, one of the goals of customer service training is to allow representatives feel as much a part of the business as you. Encourage your employees to see situations from an owner's point of view. I understand that many might be concerned about offering too many discounts or giving things away for free, but when employees can make certain good quick decisions to make customers happy without your involvement and without going through management layers, there is less aggravation for the customer.

Craig was having issues installing a component on his personal computer. After almost three hours of aggravation, he gave in and called his computer manufacturer's customer service center. It was a Saturday afternoon at 4 p.m. EST. After several moments of waiting, he was eventually transferred to Kenny. It appeared endless and both men were getting frustrated attempting to install this part. It was 72 minutes into the call when Kenny said, "Oh My." Craig said, "What is the problem—the computer?" "No," said Kenny, "they are shutting down the lights must be closing time." Craig said, "No worries, go ahead and leave I will take care of this on Monday." He was blown away at the next statement—PAUSE.

"No that is okay, you are a customer and I will do what I can to get this installed. If it takes all night," said Kenny.

Craig has since purchased four other computers from this organization.

In another situation, a customer was having a software issue. The problem was not resolved immediately but the customer service representative over the course of the next 10 days e-mailed the customer possible resolutions—on his own time and from his personal e-mail account. What works best is allowing your employees to make the important decisions so that your customers are happy, things are resolved sooner, and internally and externally all feel like they have made a difference.

There is not enough money in advertising and promotion to supplement these stories. Research proves it is 81 percent more effective to keep a happy, satisfied client than acquire a new one. Do all you can to see the business from your customer's eyes so that you can lessen barriers to customer aggravation.

Tips for Dealing with Difficult Customers

Sometimes it's important to understand that it is not the representative's fault but merely an unruly customer. Many organizations have unruly customers. It is helpful to know two things: (1) some customers do expect the world and for you to bend over backward for them no matter what and (2) some people sometimes are just rude or aggressive to others—including family so never take it personally. So let's discuss some tips about dealing with difficult clients.

First, there are issues when it comes to personality. It's important to understand that some people based upon personality and some behavioral issues will always be somewhat difficult. Take for example any of the gate agents, pilots, or even baggage handlers for any airline. In most instances, their main purpose is to get people to their destination in a safe manner. They don't control the weather, they don't control air traffic, and they don't control the many hiccups that occur. However, there are those passengers who seem to think that airlines are built for them and for no others. They get very unruly no matter what, sometimes particularly vacationers not used to delays. Simply know what you are dealing with and move on. Never take their personality personally.

Second, there are issues when conflict occurs. This is because there is a lack of information or someone has the wrong information. For example, I recently was charged $50 to have my medical records copied to a new sales professional. All I received was an invoice, no one told me; so, naturally I was ticked. Once explained, I was better.

Third, never allow issues to get personal. Customers sometimes need to vent and that is okay as long as personal feelings are not involved. Always tell your staff to never get unprofessional and if the customer is then either get help or call a time out. There is no reason for insults during a professional conversation.

Fourth, be willing to negotiate—sometimes customer service is a negotiation. Everything in life is. It is helpful to understand the art and science of negotiation. Do not worry about winning and other ideas, only that when the customer feels satisfied the issue is instantly resolved. Have your representatives ask the customer what would be an amicable settlement. Ask them what they want to receive.

Fifth, realize that customers have certain standards and no matter the rules, the customers have a perceived expectation. For example, Federal Express thrives to get packages to your door overnight. Yet, some individuals will complain when the package is not there first thing in the morning or at noon. This might be the shippers fault or bad weather, yet the customer wants it on their terms. As they say in the movies "Whata gunna do?"

Should you or your organization find that you are handling too many difficult customers and difficult situations, you might consider divorcing your clients. This may seem extreme but there are times when certain customers always complain, always want an exception, or always want a credit. At some point, this is costing more time and more money than you have. There is no reason to bow down to every request.

Just like there are bad products, bad employees, and bad companies, there are unhappy customers. It is part of business. The comedian Steve Martin in a skit once sang, "Be courteous, kind and considerate, be gentle and loving each day …" When your team is the constant professional, there is less concern about the unruly folks.

Responding Successfully to Specific Customer Expectations

If you are a lover of music as I am, then you will know the Aretha Franklin song of respect. The fact is that many customers are much more responsive and they would feel they are respected. This means that you respect their opinions, their suggestions, and even just their conversations.

Customers do not enjoy being treated differently because they have been with you for a while versus someone that is new. So in working with customers in order to help set expectations, I suggest that you show them a little bit more respect. Respect is an acronym, and I will show you how it works most effectively so that you can respond successfully.

R—Recognize repeat customers by name, or at least by face. One of the things that always boggles my mind is when vendors I have done business with for quite some time either don't remember my name or get it wrong. Drew is not a very difficult name to pronounce or remember, however, sometimes my name is Bruce or sometimes my last name is spelt with a pH. I have a friend who can walk into a room and remember almost 98 first names. So, I suggest that your staff work on techniques to remember names and qualities. You can write the names down and quiz staff, you can use software products that allow you to write personal information like birthdays and dogs' names so that staff remember. You can run contests. But do something to make it warm and personal.

E—Engage customers as soon as they enter or call. My rule of thumb about customer calls is twofold. First, always answer calls on the second or third ring. Use your first name and the department and ask how to help the client. And, respond to all calls within 90 minutes. Customers want a quick response and waiting too long in today's fast-paced world allows them to quickly log onto the Internet and keypunch or call your competitor.

S—Smile, even if you do business by phone. Constantly smile. One of my favorite books of all time is Dale Carnegie's *How to Win Friends and Influence People*. Fact number 1 is to always smile. There is no app for that. Simply smile before, during, and after your calls. Believe it or not, you can actually hear the smile because staff is more open and friendly.

P—Provide what they are looking for (whether you have it or not). Try not to make working with you so hard. To express my point, I was recently in a grocery store in my local area and asked the general manager where I could find a can of beans for a soup recipe that I was creating. He walked me through the store, down the aisle, and then asked what color I was looking for the recipe. He made suggestions but more importantly, he took me to the exact location. He made it very easy for me to find. Sometimes going out of your way to provide customers what they're looking for is exactly what is needed to create the proper customer experience. Have staff ask questions or have staff walk customers through the issue so that it is easily understood. In fact, there are software products today such as Logmein that allow you to control a client's desktop and actually show them how to control the software.

E—Enquire to find out customers' needs. One of the least used communication methods in today's society because of its quick pace is proper questioning skills. Have staff prepare questions in advance that are standard and help to quickly discover information or issues. Have them ask more than needed so that they get to the heart of the issue. You might conduct some role-play and team meetings to determine what works, what questions work best, and how to direct the customer better.

C—Check for customer satisfaction. From time to time, it is always proper to ask the customer how you were doing. There is no reason why you should be embarrassed or shy about asking the customer whether or not you are providing proper customer service. The Chase Plaza in St. Louis as well as the Ritz Carlton constantly asks their clientele whether they have done a proper job and if there is anything else they can do to make their experience happier. Even AT&T with their mobility or U-verse services constantly their calls with the simple question *have I taken care of all of your needs today*? What a great way to respond to the customer.

T—Thank them for choosing to do business with you. The easiest, but perhaps the most often overlooked is a simple thank you. If you want the customer to respond better to you, you must be more responsive to the customer. By that I mean thank them for being a customer, thank them for their patronage, and thank them for trusting you with their money and with their trust.

When you work from the eyes of the customer, you quickly seek loopholes and areas of correction to make each experience the best possible.

How to Make Customers Feel Valued and Tips for Turning One-Time Buyers into Lifetime Customers

Marriott, the hotel company, revolutionized the way employees, from desk clerks to chief financial officers, are evaluated based on guest-satisfaction scores. The result is a culture where uncommon acts of concern—such as a bellhop lending his shoes to a guest—become not so uncommon. The founders of the companies that make up Marriott's 19 brands really believe that if you take great care of your associates, they'd take great care of your customers. And when associates take care of each other, customer service goes through the roof.

Believe it or not, it is the simple things that will allow customers to return. As they say, people do judge a book by its cover. Therefore, it is important to always make a positive first impression. How do you do this? Well as an example your front desk is the first thing that speaks to and see a customer. Your front desk must answer phones, address e-mails, and have chats in a warm friendly and meaningful way. This does not mean people always have to be bubbly and charming, but they do need to show their willingness to build relationships and just care for their customers. And internally this means that all employees treat each other with professionalism and respect.

So what are some things that can make a strong impression and make customers feel valued?

- **Be concerned, be personal, be willing:** When you walk into Walgreens, Rosie is there to greet all by first name and when she does not see you for a week or so she will call or remember the very last conversation. My recommendation is for your staff to really get to know their clients, their hobbies, and their interests so they can have a good conversation about anything. Your customers will like the warmer approach.
- **Connectivity:** While we are in the electronic age, there is a need to constantly connect to customers. After all they do. Phone calls, thank you cards, and other devices are helpful in remaining in constant contact. I have a young man at a client site sending thank you cards after appointments and during some customer service issues. The great thing about this is that customers take the cards and hang them up or place them in their office showing their appreciation for your concern.
- **Delight:** Remember when you were a kid and you ate Cracker Jacks? The prize has surprised us all but today customers desire more sizzle. Customers today want to be "blown away." I was visiting Starbuck's recently and I frequently visit one particular shop. As I approached the counter, there was a Venti coffee at the register. My barista saw me coming from the parking lot, as I entered we exchanged hellos. He told me my coffee was waiting. And there was no charge. Now that is Blown Away. Have your staff do something out of

the ordinary and treat your top clients from time to time with something special such as a free coupon, a discount on service, something free like a bottle of wine, anything that is meant to surprise.

- **Discovering other ways to delight and help:** "Become a trusted person." Nordstrom used to do this when they were first expanding. Visit Nordstrom and ask for a specific tie, shoes, or cufflinks. If unavailable, the sales representative will indicate not only the closest store, but also a competitor. Sometimes when you provide something of value that can help the customer, but it does not require them buying from you actually increases customer service. The best way to do this is to keep up with customer trends in the newspapers or from service such as Mashable so that you can service them when they least expect it.

- **Addressing issues immediately:** The best advice I can provide here is to be decisive and get answers to questions quickly. Place clients on hold and get someone with the expertise needed or ask if you can research it and call back in a few moments. But no matter what, clients today like quick resolution to issues, especially when they believe they can find it with a quick Google search.

- **Return messages quickly:** Customers do not want to wait. They want answers as quickly as possible. Even Radio Shack, the electronics retailer, uses the mantra, "You have questions we have answers." Return all calls or e-mails in 24 hours. I have a policy of 90 minutes. There is a story floating around about the author and entrepreneur Guy Kawasaki, who was sent an e-mail by a potential client at 10 p.m.; he returned it 10 minutes later.

It costs eight to ten times more to gain a new client than to keep one. Providing exceptional customer service is what clients want and what they come to expect. Being customer savvy and customer exceptional is simply just good business.

Develop Service Delivery Standards
for Your Employees

I travel frequently for business. One parking facility I use personally greets me, and informs me of the exact row that I can use. I do not have to search for an open space, and if I am in their frequent parker program, they valet park me when their lot is full. I get a shuttle bus at the empty parking space. The driver helps me get my luggage out of my car and onto the bus. There is no waiting in one of those plastic shelters.

Once it was raining, and the driver met me with one of those big golf umbrellas. Most importantly—they know my first name!

One family staying at the Ritz Carlton, Bali, had carried specialized eggs and milk for their son who suffered from food allergies. Upon arrival, they saw that the eggs had broken and the milk had soured. The Ritz Carlton manager and dining staff searched the town but could not find the appropriate items. But the executive chef at this particular resort remembered a store in Singapore that sold them. He contacted his mother-in-law, and asked that she buy the products and fly to Bali to deliver them, which she agreed to do. Of course the family was delighted.

After doing some research, I have discovered that the key to effective customer service is practicing it. I have found over the course of time that physicians practice, lawyers practice; musicians practice; and even athletes practice. Each of them goes about their day practicing to ensure success toward an end result. Business people therefore must practice too.

I developed a proprietary formula known as PRACTICE to assist you with some simple practice standards.

- PRACTICE starts with a P-Positive first impression ...
  Insist on a Positive First Impression—you must be genuinely interested in assisting others. Passion and empathy separates the athletes from the spectators. These include warm greetings on the telephone or direct. Being positive gets things moving in the proper direction. The Four Seasons ensures that every guest is greeted enthusiastically with each and every interaction.
- The R in PRACTICE is rapport ... Develop Rapport—98 percent of every interaction involves trust and respect. Ensure

you establish rapport with every client. Your call center is only as good as your back-end operation. If a representative tells a customer that a package will be shipped in two days, make sure your distribution center fulfills that promise. Check with distribution and call the client to ensure it has arrived.

- A in PRACTICE Assesses the Issue—Ask the proper questions to totally understand the issue. One of the things noticeable on many chat calls or customer service centers is that service representatives actually ask the client to replicate and explain the issue. So if the television stopped working, ask the clients what they were doing before, during, and after the issue occurred. Reproduce so you can diagnose.

- C in PRACTICE Communicate fully and thoroughly with Communication—The best communicators listen first and speak second. Athletes know when to ask and when to tell. We all like to diagnose issues and begin explaining information. But when it comes to service representatives, they need to speak less and listen more. First your customers want to vent and express their concern. Second, THEY want to tell you about the issue and then THEY want to tell you when they want it fixed. Tell staff to settle back and listen and do not rush the call.

- T in PRACTICE is Time ... Manage time effectively is Time Management—Customer Service representatives are trained to expeditiously respond to issues but can you do this qualitatively too? I know of one client that uses e-mail to express client issues, however, they use no welcoming message and no conclusion and they also do not use an action step. Ensure that staff use proper e-mail protocols such as an opening line, a summary of the issue, the steps to resolve the issue, and the action steps needed along with a conclusion. Phone calls must be similar. Use a template to ensure that customers do not feel rushed.

- I in PRACTICE is interest ... Take an Interest—Taking interest means building rapport and have a nice pleasant conversation with each customer. It means attempting to build trust internally and externally. Two ways to do this are first internally—get to know others in other departments that you need to work with daily, whether it is accounts receivable, sales, shipping, the help desk, finance who-ever. Now I recognize this might be difficult in today's virtual organization, but simply visiting another person in another department or picking up the phone and making an introduction is all that is needed to be more internally service savvy. Externally, it means not only going the extra mile to build a relationship, but also actually showing concern for the issue. For example, there was a time I checked into a hotel in Dallas and it was completely sold out. I had a reservation but the hotel was double booked. Worse yet, it was 1 a.m. in the morning and my flight was delayed. You will not believe what happened next, the hotel clerk called another hotel that he thought might have a reservation and then ordered a bellhop to walk me five blocks with my baggage to the other hotel. Every time I visit Dallas, I stay at the original hotel because of their supreme concern of taking an interest.

- C in PRACTICE … Close on a Positive Note—Always close your calls on the positive side seeking to address any open issues and questions. And ask the customer if you have resolved the issue.

- And E in PRACTICE … Evaluate what's going on … Ensure you evaluate every customer interaction—Customer service requires conviction and passion to aid others. Once complete with your calls, ensure you also evaluate to carry these themes from call to call. I recommend weekly call report meetings to look for trends, see what the gaps in service were, and how quickly information was resolved. Try to resolve repeated issues and do not worry about too many anomalies.

Measure and Assess How Well Customer Service Standards Are Being Achieved

Data are vital to every customer service program. It is necessary to deal in data, analyze them, and then use them to become better. Research is always necessary to help understand the data points for customer service.

The one problem, however, with most organizations is that data tend to sit in a database. It is then necessary that senior management, owners, and all personnel become involved in not only gathering data, but also analyzing them.

Fact-finding is a large part of what the Girl Scouts do on a day-to-day basis. Even the Society of Human Resource Management routinely conducts leadership and advertising surveys, member needs assessment, and other surveys to better understand the issues of its members. After all, the association is run by its members.

So the question then is how do you measure customer service? This can be done in several ways.

First, it is easy to measure service by reviewing the level of customer service calls. As customer service issues are resolved, representatives are handling less troublesome calls. Use a spreadsheet or software to determine how many calls you handle and where there are repeated service issues.

Second, develop customer focus groups. Customer focus groups are investigative research events where up to 10 customers meet under the guidance of an expert facilitator to discuss their service experiences, their views, feelings, and opinions in an open forum.

Customer focus groups are a useful way of establishing a comprehensive range of opinions on customer values, assumptions, and beliefs about the service you provide as well as looking at future service offerings and improvements. They are particularly helpful among consumer markets and can also be used in business-to-business environments. What is necessary is inviting your clients to a small meeting with a fixed agenda and where they can meet some members of senior staff to voice trends, provide issues, and illustrate concerns in your organization's processes. You need to offer a personal invitation on a voluntary basis and also provide follow-ups after the meeting to resolve open issues.

Fourth, surveys are very good with getting insight about customer service. Do not just look at numbers and statistics, but also qualitative feedback and what is being mentioned by consumers. I recommend the use of Likert Surveys, which are those one to five choices that not only ask about your average, above average, or below average performance, but also enable the customer to supply qualitative information so you can "hear" the meaning of the numbers.

Finally, *every customer evaluates* his or her experience buying a product or service. A tool used to measure the quality of that experience is mystery shopping. Hired as independent contractors, mystery shoppers are "posers" operating in stealth-like fashion to assess your business operations. They are charged with specific tasks such as taking photographs, purchasing a product or service, returning a product, registering complaints, asking questions of sales representatives, and behaving in other ways. Mystery shopping can be applied in any industry, although the more common venues are retail stores, restaurants, banks, hotels, car dealerships, and health-care facilities. But any company that has a customer can benefit from having a mystery shopping program.

Mystery shoppers check service, layout, ambience, adherence to guidelines, and store or restaurant displays during their visit. Prepare a checklist of the items upon which you need to report. Store the checklist on your smartphone, in your pocket, or purse to ensure you get proper credit for your mystery shopping work.

For example, during the mystery shopping visit, you typically need to note the number of staff, the items on display, whether a particular item is highlighted, and how quickly after entry you are greeted and helped. Glance at your watch or phone when you enter and check it again after you're asked if you need assistance. When conducting a restaurant visit, timing is particularly important. You need to note the appearance of the restaurant, track the time you are seated, when your server arrives, how quickly an order is taken, and the time lapse between ordering and receiving the components of the meal: appetizer, main course, and dessert, if ordered.

Great service is not just about speed and accuracy, but also about warmth and personalization. Service is important with all aspects of your company so you must get them involved.

Ironically, customer service is part of every organization, product, and service including the government. Yes yours truly has even been sent to the United States Postal Service to aid in their customer service efforts. As much as selling affects every organization, customer service has an even more profound impact. Unfortunately, many organizations are chastised and condemned for poor customer service. Yet with every bad story there are also numerous grand stories.

The simplest thing about customer service is that if you treat customers with professionalism and empathy they will continually return. They will tell others. Customer service is the key to your marketing and profitability success factors. It lowers attrition in organization and it heightens productivity.

What is now required is simply to start building those relationships. As I mentioned at the beginning of this chapter, which is easier for you: (a) chipping away at 50 or 60 cold calls every day in getting a high degree of negativity in zero return or (b)simply picking up the phone and say hello, this is_____, how may I assist you today?

Best practices in action steps are as follows:

- Return of calls, text messages, and e-mails within 90 minutes of receipt. I utilize this in my practice and I cannot tell you how many times people call or e-mail and tell me I have 89 minutes and they're waiting. Potential consumers want to challenge salespeople to illustrate whether they are responsive or not.
- Use handwritten notes to say thank you from meeting individuals or for the order. Believe it or not, in today's electronic age, a handwritten note will last forever. Don't believe me? Visit your next client and look on the credenza with a desk and see whether or not your competitors have conducted this vital exercise.
- Hire a friend or colleague to review your sales interactions. Or, record some of your sales calls on video or audio utilizing your smartphone. What items would you change during your interaction? What questions might you ask that you didn't? What things might you have done to create better service your perspective client?
- When possible make decisive decisions. Don't tell people that you are going to get back to your manager or you need to check on something. Inform the client that you're going to take care of it personally. You need to feel empowered to create better customer service.

- Look at the processes that you have in place when it comes to your interactions with clients. What one or two things might you be able to do to create a more streamlined process? Think in terms of the local Subway restaurant or even Jimmy John's. Both organizations make ordering a sandwich exceedingly easy. What can you do to streamline the operations of your business?
- Use your existing customer relationship management software or purchase one, so that you can make notes of your clients and recall names, historical events, or any other item necessary in creating a better relationship with your client.

Just a quick word before you turn the page. In this particular chapter, we talked about customer service but the implication was about relationships. Building those relationships will be key to every selling professional's success. And, one of the most terrific methods building relationships is networking. Networking is nothing more than meeting new people who might be able to provide referrals or perhaps become new clients. The more you engage in this notion of building relationships, the better you will be and extending your reach to individuals who will become interested in the products and services that you have. So let's read on and show you how to build a network of individuals to become instantly attracted to you like a spider in a net. When you have developed this formulaic approach, you'll never have to make another cold call again!

CHAPTER 5

Networking Skills—Keys to Pipeline Success

Business networking is the process of meeting other people and exchanging resources for mutual gain. Business networking forms the basis of business relationships. Selling professionals rely heavily upon effective networking practices to win clients and partners. Your ability to network well is one of the factors that may not only differentiate your practice, but also ensure its survival.

Networking is one of those skills that you need to acquire in order to develop relationships with individuals who could potentially lead you to new forms of business. If I may ask you which is going to be easier: making 500 calls to get a yes or being in a room with 50 people who perhaps understand your value and could potentially tell another 200? The latter is the obvious choice. I understand that networking is not easy for those who are introverted or don't enjoy the social atmospheres of group interaction. However, there is a notion in our contemporary society of "one-to-many" approach. For too many years, selling professionals have attempted to reach their potential markets by making one phone call, directing one meeting, or traveling to one individual. This creates a huge investment in time and a very large gap in return on investment. Nowadays, I instruct selling professionals to take a one-to-many approach to help lessen the labor and increase the return rates. Networking is one of those skilled approaches, whereby you might be speaking with 30 to 50 people, or even 6 who could become interested in the products and services that you sell. The returns are easier because you have a group rather than one individual. So let's take a quick look at the value of networking and how to quickly build up your war chest of referrals and prospective opportunities.

The problem with networking is that many selling professionals don't enjoy it because it takes them from their comfort zone and most importantly treatment. Most people are more comfortable conversing with those they know and meeting new people is simply an annoyance.

However, meeting new people has three positive effects:

- Lessen labor—meeting new individuals allows you to prospect less as more individuals get to know you.
- Increases productivity—the more individuals you meet the more often you express your value to others.
- Increases visibility—the more you network, the more visible you will be.

To help express my point, Michael Douglass and Charlie Sheen before he went ballistic on television starred in a wonderful movie called *Wall Street*. Sheen's character Bud Fox wanted to become a Wall Street Maverick. He wanted to bag elephants like Michael Douglass—Wall Street millionaire and iconic trader and Fox would do anything to do so. He went to events, cold called him—literally anything to meet the tycoon. And when he did, he was introduced to others and began to make thousands if not millions for himself. This is why networking is so vital to success.

Networking Mindset

You can go to all of the networking meetings under the sun and collect hundreds of business cards, while you're at it but if you're not hanging out with people you can do business with, you might make some new friends, you won't necessarily grow your business.

If you want to grow your practice by networking, it is imperative that you network with: people who are your ideal clients, people who know your ideal clients, and people who do business with your ideal clients. It's that simple. When you network with people who need your services (or know others who do), there will be a natural interest in knowing more about your business.

Here are some things to consider:

- Effective networking can increase your visibility and strengthen your career. The more people you meet, the more they know you. The most successful people in the world have vast networks. These help with jobs, leads, aid, and a whole lot more.
- Do not be a wallflower, make networking productive. In order to receive, you have to give. Sitting in a corner and being inactive does not make you a networker. Even flour must be kneaded before it is made into bread, you have to work at it.
- Remember to use an audio logo or value proposition. I work with many business owners and selling professionals. When I ask them what they do, they immediately rush into their title, stating, "I am the president of a bank," "I am a consultant," or "I am a professional speaker." If I were a client and heard this, I would immediately think, "So what?" Great networkers refrain from using their titles and occupations and instead provide an answer to the question "So what?" The method for doing this is known as a value proposition. Simply put, a value proposition is a statement that promotes the business to clients using outcome and results. This brief statement denotes the benefit(s) that a client receives from working with you. It is outcome based and focuses all attention on client.
- Think relationship not transaction—A myth of networking is geared to the transactional end meaning that many attend expecting immediate business. Networking is about creating relationships that build trust and respect. The notion is to become a trusted advisor, this does not happen overnight.
- Networking is a process and it takes at least six months of concentrated effort to build.
- While networking has always been vital to business relationships and growing a client base, it's never been quite as easy as it is now. While face-to-face interaction remains the best form of networking, you no longer need to rely on snail

mail or even phone calls to interact and create a group. With social networking sites, you can research and connect with other professionals easier than ever.

I typically suggest that to network effectively, we must engage in something known as the four Es.

- Enjoy the moment. Networking is making the most of small talk.
- Engage is a satisfying relationship with each other. Get beyond the superficial routines.
- Exchange valuable information. Be aware of what the speaker is looking for. Ask probing questions to know their challenges. Give information, and then get some in return. Know what information you're looking for.
- Explore future opportunities. Develop a good relationship for the future. Networking isn't the time for either of you to get deep into a project.

As we all know, networking is a powerful way of building professional relationships and generating new business opportunities. It is a reciprocal process based on the exchange of ideas, advice, contacts, and referrals. Although there is no one-size-fits-all way to network, it is important to remember proper business etiquette when approaching and developing new professional relationships.

Apply the right business networking techniques and you could be well on your way to growing your small business, but get it wrong and you'll be left wondering why others are successful with their networking.

- Schedule a meeting immediately. A networking event should not be viewed as an opportunity to fill up your calendar. It is more advantageous to get to know people first before taking out your smartphone or tablet device. By acting too eager you may be perceived as looking at other participants only as dollar signs. If a connection is made, ask for permission to call or e-mail them within a specific time frame. ("Would you mind if I called you early next week to set up an appointment to continue our conversation?")

- Monopolize their time. Everyone attending an event is looking to increase his or her networking base. When you monopolize someone's time, they are unavailable to meet new people. Be considerate and spend only two to five minutes with each person than move on. If someone corners you for too long, politely disengage by saying "It has been such a pleasure talking to you, but I'm sure there are other people here you'd like to meet."

- Name drop. You may know many people that networkers want to get acquainted with, but this will eventually come out in conversation once you determine whom the networker would like to meet. Bragging about people you know turns others off.

- Ask personal questions. If you have just met a person, it does not show the best judgment to ask how much money they make, their marital status, what religion they follow, or how old they are. If a future business exchange requires personal information, then it should be done in follow-up conversations. Keep the mood light and interesting.

You Have Three Seconds to Make a First Impression

We have all heard this warning: "You never get a second chance to make a good first impression." I have read that we only have 7 to 17 seconds of interacting with strangers before they form an opinion of us. In fact, in today's fast moving environment where 140-word tweets and even shorter text messages are the standard mode of communication, you now only have three seconds to grab a person's attention. First impression is important because this is what people use to make judgments—good or bad.

The following example will illustrate my point: In 1980, John Hurt starred as John Merrick, the hideously deformed 19th century Londoner known as "The Elephant Man." Although part of a circus sideshow, he was very intelligent but Merrick was still treated like a freak; no matter his station in life, he will forever be a prisoner of his own malformed body.

The greatest way to make a positive first impression is to demonstrate immediately that the other person, not you, is the center of action and conversation. Illustrate that the spotlight is on you only, and you'll miss opportunities for friendships, jobs, love relationships, networking, and sales. Show that you are other-centered, and first-time acquaintances will be eager to see you again.

- Visuals matter: dress appropriateness, neatness, hygiene, posture, eye contact, and smile. In the age of "Dress-Down Friday" and Internet Frump, what's appropriate to wear to work? In many companies, there are no carved-in-stone rules, so when in doubt, go traditional. While operating a seminar recently, I had a gentleman question me about a statement I made about using pens and having good tools such as padfolios and briefcases. I stated that all should run out and buy a good pen, watch, and briefcase. His question verbatim, "Do you think that the guy I am negotiating a deal with gives a care about the pen I am using." My reply, you are a selling professional with incredible healing power. I would hope to death that you would use a Mont Blanc and not a 1.99 pen to illustrate your implication of professionalism. Be the consummate professional. This means dressing well, hiding tattoos and piercings, as well as being professionally groomed with good clothes and those that fit well.
- Nonverbal behaviors, such as handshake, posture, personal space, and facial gestures influence others. Messages can be communicated through gestures and touch, by body language or posture, by facial expression, and by eye contact. Meaning can also be communicated through object or artifacts (such as clothing, hairstyles, or architecture). Speech contains nonverbal elements known as paralanguage, including voice quality, rate, pitch, volume, and speaking style, as well as prosodic features such as rhythm, intonation, and stress. Dance is also regarded as a form of nonverbal communication. What messages does your body send? Be cautious so that the desired message is delivered.

- Remember the priority: Take an interest in the most important person in the conversation, the other person. One of the keys, if not the most important one, to building successful relationships is your ability to show a sincere interest—both in the person and things that are important to that person. By expressing genuine interest in someone's qualities, background, stories, hobbies, career, family, or anything else closely connected to that person, you will give them a gift—a sense of importance, well-being, and value. *Patch Adams* is the movie about a nonconventional physician who cares about one thing—the health and welfare of his clients. Patch speaks, cajoles, and laughs with the clients and have them speak about their loves, likes, and strengths. He takes in everything while offering very little about himself. They love him because of his intense interest in others.
- Listen with interest: There is a difference between simply listening to people and listening with deep interest. Listening with interest signifies that you really care about what they are saying in contrast to simply listening because it is the polite thing to do. If you question whether people can tell the difference, Don't. They can and they will readily make judgments about you if they sense you are pretending to listen.
- Ask questions to encourage dialogue. A great way to demonstrate interest is to ask questions. It could be as simple as striking up a conversation with a coworker about what they did over the weekend. Or perhaps asking something about the person's family. Asking questions generally stimulates a person to talk about their interests and themselves.

The key to leaving a lasting impression is to find ways that allow you to continue to build the relationship with this person in your network.

If you want to leave a positive lasting impression with those you work with, socialize with, or have a close relationship with, you need to decide what qualities you want to be remembered for. Do you want them to remember you as efficient, organized, and dedicated to your job? Do you want them to remember you as passionate about your dreams, committed to a cause, and one who always looks for the positive in a situation? Do you want to leave a lasting impression that reminds others of the important role you played in their life?

Perhaps the best way to leave a lasting impression is to live each day as if your actions that day will be what comes to mind when people think of you. From the first impression you make to the lasting impression you wish to leave, try to present yourself as self-confident, positive, unique, and genuine.

Author Ralph Waldo Emerson said it best: "Do not go where the path may lead, go instead where there is no path, and leave a trail."

Here are some simple tips about a lasting impression:

1. Capture them permanently in your personal database—so easy with today's technology, even business card scanners.
2. Add them to your networks online (LinkedIn, Facebook, etc.).
3. Follow through with commitments (introductions, information, etc.) in a timely manner—make note before you leave, never be without a pen and paper.
4. "Touch" them consistently within appropriate time spaces—the key to leaving a lasting impression is doing what you say you're going to do.
5. Call to check-in or thank them … or to pass on an idea/additional information.
6. E-mail information they will find interesting/beneficial.
7. Offer additional insights into you—"I was thinking about our last conversation and something occurred to me. You wouldn't know that I have a past career in … this might be helpful to you as you move forward on that project we were discussing."

I also suggest that you let others talk. Asking questions is a great way to uncover needs that another business might have. By simply asking about and understanding their issues, your company may be able to assist them in accomplishing their goals. For example, many businesses are seeking to enhance their health and wellness benefits. Asking an individual what they're already doing will identify what they're not doing, and can be extremely beneficial in devising a plan. Get as much information as possible in order to uncover any areas your practice might be able to assist with.

Make it personal. The fact is, networking isn't strictly business. We have to enjoy it and be excited to meet interesting new people. Finding out about people on a personal level will enhance any future interactions, relationships, and make the whole process much more fun. You will likely connect with people based on a similar interest such as kids, a sport, a hobby, or a hometown. People light up when talking about their personal passions.

The Power of Presence

One way to leverage the power of presence is to leverage the skill of charisma. Charisma is the impression you make in the mind of others. The impression you leave will have a lot to do with the skills you develop. Do you remember the movie *Pretty Women* with Julia Roberts? When she first showed up at the retail stores on Rodeo Drive, all the shopkeepers ignored her. She was common, she was unsophisticated, and she lacked charisma. But then Richard Gere took her shopping, gave her a new look and feel, and then ... Wha la.

Another example is Mahatma Gandhi, he had no army. He never accepted any political office. He never used violence. He never threatened with violence. He was a small, frail, little man. Yet he defeated the armed might of the British Empire. He drove the British out of India without firing a single shot. How did he do it? Personal Presence. Personal Presence will allow you to move mountains if you need to.

The first impression you make on others can easily be influenced by your visual, nonverbal gestures and posture, personal presence, and ability to make and receive introductions.

The quality of self-assurance and effectiveness permits a performer to achieve a rapport with the audience. An appealing physical appearance doesn't mean that you have to have movie-star looks or spend a fortune on clothes, but it does mean that you need to dress appropriately and professionally. Your appearance sends a message about who you are. You might not be able to judge a book by its cover, but, whether you like it or not, people will judge you by what you look like. In this age of attention to diversity, this might sound politically incorrect, but if you want to draw people to you, you need to show up in a powerful way that attracts a majority of people. Therefore, pay attention to the message your clothes and appearance send. Think for a moment about the presence that a millionaire gives off and that of a homeless person. Notice the shoulders, the way the clothes lay on the body, the speech, and so on. People are turned on and off to presence like a light switch.

A person with poise has the capacity to draw the eyes of everyone in a room. Having this trait attracts not only attention, but also the admiration of many who long to be equally put together, confident, and assured. A person with poise can start a conversation with ease, listen in a relaxed manner, and come across as both laid-back and sophisticated. If you want to be more poised stand up tall with your shoulders back, show a level of confidence. Standing tall also shows you are confident as well as approachable. Additionally, you might want to illustrate some good etiquette. Learning your manners is one of the most essential ways to have poise. It is difficult for someone who is clumsy at the dinner table to be considered sophisticated; having poise is not about drawing undue attention to oneself. Understanding proper manners will keep the attention on what matters and demonstrate your awareness of the proper etiquette when it comes to important events. Please, thank you, holding doors and chairs are great ways to illustrate your poise.

And remember, professionalism is about how you speak and how you dress. You must be comfortable in your clothes and in your own skin.

- Personality
- Body language
- Handshake
- Dress

You must also remember to:

Control the Impression You Make

You also have an aura around you that most people cannot see but that is there, nevertheless. This aura affects the way people react and respond to you, either positively or negatively. There is a lot that you can do, and a lot of good reasons for you to do it, to control this aura and make it work in your best interests.

Influence People Around You

If you're in business, developing greater charisma can help you tremendously in working with your staff, your suppliers, your bankers, your clients, and everyone else upon whom you depend for your success. People seem naturally drawn to those who possess charisma.

They want to help them and support them. When you have charisma, people will open doors for you and bring you opportunities that otherwise would not have been available to you.

In your personal relationships, the quality of charisma can make your life more joyous and happier. People will naturally want to be around you. Members of your family and your friends will be far happier in your company, and you will have a greater influence on them, causing them to feel better about themselves and to do better at the important things in their lives.

One of the things to remember about networking is to offer some positioning and thought leadership so people not only come to know you, but also become more attracted to you.

- You are able to change others' perspectives.
- You are constantly teaching others, formally and informally.
- You coin phrases, metaphors, concepts, and models which others quickly embrace.
- You make the complex simple and pragmatic (instantiation).
- Every knowledgeable person in your field or niche knows you, whether they agree with you or not.
- You have an impressive array of examples, applications, war stories, and a substantial track record of success.
- You dress professionally.
- You use good vocabulary.
- You are well read.
- You are well researched.

Best Practice—the Follow-up

When you attend a networking event, whether a conference, seminar, or business-club meeting, your work has just begun. It's the follow-up after the event that can really pay dividends for you. This includes trading information that is valuable to each other over e-mail and gaining extended connections from a single contact. Too many people walk away from networking events feeling good but doing nothing.

1. Introduce two people to one another.

   Find someone at an event and introduce them to other parties. When you do this, it helps to extend your network and allows you the opportunity to grow referrals and aid additional times opportunities to meet new people.

2. Send an e-mail, no later than 24 hours.

   Don't wait until the next day or the next week. Chances are you won't get around to it, and even if you do, the recipient may not recall who you are. You need to send an e-mail to everyone you took a card from. Even if you don't see an immediate connection, just say thanks. And I also recommend sending a personal thank you card on your own stationery.

3. Seek referrals.

   One of the best ways to grow both a business and a network is by collaborating with others. Joint ventures can be amazingly powerful; anytime I network I attempt to seek out one referral partner.

4. Make notes on your experiences.

   Bullet-point ideas, or write them across your whiteboard. Just get them down!

5. Check your website.

   If you have a website, make sure it's working well and the links are active. If you meet a lot of people, chances are some will check out your website. Make sure that it is up-to-date and a good representation of who you are.

As social networking sites such as LinkedIn, Facebook, and Twitter grow in popularity, we tend to forget about that "old-fashioned" approach to networking: face-to-face contact. Sure, it's a lot easier to sit behind the computer all day and network using the point-and-click method. But if you want to expand your network, you must be very visible and very active before and after.

The key to leaving a lasting impression is to find ways that allow you to continue to build the relationship with this person in your network. To exemplify my point, *Schindler's List* is a 1993 American film about Oskar Schindler, a German businessman who saved the lives of more than a thousand mostly Polish-Jewish refugees during the Holocaust by employing them in his factories. As one watches the film, they notice the ability of Oskar Schindler to speak and interact with many in the movie. Whether it is with the Jewish people or the Nazi SS officers, Mr. Schindler has a way to provide a very interesting impression with his piercing eyes, his commanding presence, and his ability to question and interact with practically anyone he meets. The use of networking allows him ways to find the right people who make the decisions for him to save Jews. And when he meets individuals, they remember him even months after the first meeting. When you make an indelible first impression, you immediately decrease barriers to help build your network and aid your future performance. When you remove yourself from the comfort zone and allow yourself the opportunity to meet and greet new individuals, you will make the most out of networking.

Best practices in action steps are as follows:

- Visit only networking events where potential buyers will be located. Stop attending events with peers and colleagues. The idea behind networking is to meet individuals who could potentially use your products and services and not create new friends or share stories with present ones.
- Visit networking events alone. This places you in the most vulnerable position so that you have to meet new people.
- Never arrive late to a networking event. Every networking opportunity has the first 30 minutes of individuals interacting with each other. Arriving late eliminates your opportunity to do so.
- Eliminate the transactional side of networking. Too many individuals at networking events bring their business cards in the hopes of selling the business cards, flowers, real estate

opportunities, and a myriad of other things. You'll make yourself different by asking intelligent questions of the other party so that you illustrate value and the focus is all on that other party and not you.

- Follow-up on every opportunity. Call individuals a day or two after the networking event and invite them for coffee or a quick lunch. The opportunity to meet people outside the networking event will help to build your referral base and potential client base.

- I mentioned before about being nontransactional, but most important is to ask questions. Never hijack a relationship by speaking about you. Make sure that you do not step on sentences, make statements such as "such a thing happen to me" or take over where there was a pause in the person's sentence. Let that person tell you everything about him or her.

- Dress for success. Make sure you understand the protocol of the dress code and dress your best so that you impress every individual that you meet. Ensure that your presence brings opportunities to you.

- Make a goal for every networking event. In other words, have an idea of how many people you're going to meet, how many business cards you're going to collect, and how many people you're going to follow-up with. Treat every networking event as an opportunity to progress your small enterprise.

- Don't think that social media is the only way to the network. People even in today's contemporary world are taken in by direct interaction. Take the time to get out and meet people directly so that you can share ideas and they can understand your value.

A quick word about this chapter can be a prelude to the next. In this particular chapter, we talked about building your business network so that you can develop a war chest of future opportunities. This includes meeting as many individuals as possible so that you never have to make another cold call again. I recall an insurance agent who asked for three to five referrals on every call he made. Imagine that if you visited 100 clients and obtained 3 names per client. The total names provided is 300, which are more names collected than if you were to cold call or attempt to directly meet this many people. All he needed to do was pick up the phone and say, "Is this Ted, Roger Simons suggested I call you and that you would be interested in the value I have to provide." And imagine if 40 of those calls became clients. Now that's a nice little safety net in a comfortable commission check. Therefore, it is vital that you use networking to extend relationships. Yet, part of the networking experience is also asking the people that you conduct business with or those who understand your value for a referral. A referral is nothing more than the name of an individual or a group of individuals who would be interested in the value that you provide to your established customer base. Referrals are considered the "low-hanging fruit" and not enough selling professionals seek them out. Whether you are just a true selling professional or even a consultant being grossly immersed in the referrals business can make you an extremely successful professional; and one who can retire early and one who can have substantial financial gain. So let's read on and illustrate how you can develop your new savings account!

CHAPTER 6

The Holy Grail of Referrals

One of the key influencers for any seller is the number of referrals obtained from customers. Referrals are the hallmark to every successful sales because they provide testimonials from happy customers. Customers referring you to their friends, colleagues, and peers are the ultimate sign of trust and respect; the biggest compliment that any client can provide to a selling professional is a referral.

The chief concern about referrals is how well you build client relationships. Sales development today is achieved with a considerable focus on value and client deliverables. In our competitive society, client-to-client influences are exceedingly strong. Customers today demand relationships. What needs to be understood is that we are in a service-based economy. With that in mind, it is imperative that considerable focus be placed on client relationships. This is consistent with many of the theories of this book. As mentioned previously, the purpose of any seller is to acquire and retain customers. When retention rates are high, customers are more apt to tell others of the value they receive from the selling professional.

Referrals are linked to client loyalty. And customers are inextricably linked to sales value. As loyalty grows among your client base, so does the number of referrals.

Case Study

Charlie had been in sales for five years and was concerned about marketing and advertising costs. After reading a periodical article on referrals, he decided to begin the process. Having followed the example of a copier representative from years before, he was able to build a significant income in just a few short months. Rather than solicit one referral from a client, Charlie thought it best to ask for multiples. He asked each of his 120 customers for four referrals. He asked for 10 months and had well over 3,200 referrals before year-end. Even if he had closed two percent of his sales, he still had more opportunities than he would have had if he had chosen traditional marketing routes.

Many organizations dismiss referrals. Because entrepreneurs and other business professionals are so busy, they often forget to ask for them. However, referrals decrease costs while increasing lead generation possibilities.

We currently live in a world where customer-to-customer influences are extremely vital. It was only 10 to 15 years ago when consumers needing products or services researched using the Yellow Pages. Today, consumers typically use the Internet and search engines such as Google to find information about required products and services. They typically seek counsel from friends, colleagues, and peers who have done business with needed vendors. The rationale here is that consumers want to immediately trust those that you trust. For example, if your parent or immediate family member were ill, would it be more useful to look up a position in the Yellow Pages, conduct an Internet search, or simply call someone you trust?

In addition, with the increased use of social networks, consumers are speaking positively and negatively about vendors they have done business with. Therefore, it is imperative that if you sell for a living you ensure that your name and brand are in good standing so that you can obtain third-party endorsements from those who trust you.

Dispelling the Myths of Referrals

Many entrepreneurs and business professionals believe that they do not have enough time to obtain referrals. This could not be further from the truth. If consumers are happy in doing business with you, they are more apt to give you a referral. All you must do is ask. Later in this chapter, I will provide you with the tools necessary to help you ask for those referrals. For now, just remember that if you want a referral, you need to ask.

Second, there are those who believe if you do a good job, a consumer is more than likely to provide you with referrals. This is not so. If you want a referral, you need to ask. Never make an assumption in business for which you truly do not know the answer. The only way for a consumer to provide you with a referral is for them to see the value and for you to ask for it.

Third, there are some individuals who believe that referrals lead to nothing. In other words, there is no correlation to future business. That may or may not be true. Just because you've received a referral from a present client, this does not guarantee business. The referral needs to be worked just like any new prospect.

Fourth, many individuals believe that getting referrals is easy. This also is false. Referrals are obtained only when a present or former client truly understands the value that you provide and promotes that to others. Referrals are not an easy business; they are merely a gateway to newer opportunities. Using referrals circumvents your need to spend obscene amounts of money on marketing and advertising to obtain leads.

When to Ask for a Referral

One of the biggest mistakes when trying to obtain a referral is deciding when. Most business professionals typically wait for the conclusion of the sale, and days and weeks after, before even asking. If you want business you need to ask for it. Those who are passive do not get what they seek. Those who are more proactive will get what they want every time.

Proactivity means asking the client for a referral at the moment of *value impact*. Value impact is that moment when the client understands the value that you provide and is ready and willing to do business with you. You understand the objectives that need to be delivered and the client sees the return on investment from your value. This is the best time to ask because the sale has hit its peak. Waiting until after contract signature, invoicing, or any other post-sale meeting provides too much time for cognitive dissonance. This is the time when clients think negatively about the product or service and might want to change their mind.

In this segment, I want to focus on what to say so that you can get the best exposure and offer the most value to your clients.

I suggest using the following wording verbatim or practicing a similar vocabulary until you feel comfortable enough with a client. It is best to be comfortable yet confident so that you get the desired reward.

"Dear Mr./Mrs. _____

Today's competitive economy presents a myriad of challenges to business growth. However, as you know, the bedrock of every business is the admiration and support from clients like you. Business is built on the foundation of clients who appreciate the value that we provide. I would like to ask you for the names of three to five friends, colleagues, or peers who might be in need and appreciative of the value that I can provide to their organization.

I would like the opportunity to call you in the next few days to obtain these names so that I can continue to build my business and foster new relationships similar to ours.

I thank you so much in advance and look forward to speaking with you."

This model illustrates three vital components:

1. The value of your existing relationship
2. The importance of the continued relationship
3. The appreciation of your value and how it can be perceived by others

Clients who feel so strongly about the relationship and value will be more than happy to provide you with the names of others who can extend the loyalty and admiration. Remember, you must be confident and articulate clearly yet succinctly what you seek. I also suggest not beating around the bush. Make the statement, pause, and then listen intently. Allow your client time to process the request to consider how to assist you.

One final point. Do not end the conversation without having received what you seek. Allowing too much time between the initial request and its conclusion will create dissonance. And in today's busy world, you may not get another opportunity to ask a similar request.

Referral building depends on value and the best evidence of this is through customer service. Research illustrates that between 45 and 60 percent of every customer interaction involves customer service. The key differentiator in a competitive environment is the quality of service customers receive when doing business with your organization.

It is widely known that customers are 18 percent more likely to remain with organizations that treat them well. Customer service clearly reduces expenses when current clients remain with the firm due to loyalty. Most important, customers help to acquire new clients by becoming marketing avatars. Loyalty has a lot to do with how well companies deliver on their basic promises.

When customers believe that they are treated fairly and have a marginal equity in the organization, they become loyalists. Loyalty and value are directly correlated to customer referrals. Please note that I am not merely speaking of the customary customer referral programs, but the true level of appreciation of clients who have been doing business with you. When clients believe in you they will refer other clients. For example, if your local barber or pharmacist did something for you during each visit that saves you time and money, you might be more tempted to tell all of your friends about the fabulous experience. Or you might even bring some of your friends with you on your next visit.

This clever form of customer acquisition is known as a referral program. While many organizations use a formal referral program such as punch cards or stamps, nothing is better for increased business than a loyal customer telling others. According to a study in the *Journal of Marketing*, customer referral programs are indeed a financially attractive way for firms to acquire new customers. These value-based programs illustrate that good referrals from existing customers generate higher margins than any other customer program. Customer referral programs stemming from a culture of customer service have even higher gains than any other organization. Simply put, loyal customers generate more revenue at a lower cost to the firm and any traditional marketing approach. It is therefore imperative that organizations become more proficient and embed customer service in their culture; this lowers expenses and produces more profits while lowering acquisition costs.

Activities to Help Gain Additional Referrals

Several traditional and nontraditional resources for creating a referral network are available. Some traditional resources are sending gift cards or writing letters to clients. Many individuals still send handwritten notes and greeting cards to their clients. Keep track of anniversaries, birthdays, or other noteworthy announcements. Customer relationship management software facilitates this process. Electronic delivery does not require constant use of electronics.

However, if lack of time affects the ability to remain in constant contact, other resources are available. Business professionals can use a wealth of electronic sources to assist them. Some of these include e-mail marketing campaigns, electronic newsletters, electronic tip sheets, and even electronic greeting cards. "SendOutCards" is a relatively new service. Simply upload your database into their Internet software and choose a greeting card of your choice. This service then uses your electronic signature and manually mails the card to your customer. This is a great service if you lack the time and energy to sign and mail an important announcement. No matter what you do, remain focused on your client. Most important, it is imperative that your clients appreciate your value and can articulate it to prospective clients. Remember, "Out of sight out of mind." To build up your referral network, you must remain in harmony with customers.

Best Practices and Action Steps

- Make it easy: Allow others to know your value. It is beneficial for you to develop a value proposition so that others can repeat your value to others within their community. For more information on creating a value proposition, see Review pages 91 to 94 in this book.
- Remain in contact: I mentioned earlier that in order to get referrals, you must remain in constant contact with your customer base. If you do not, your competitor will.
- Communicate often: Ensure you're communicating with your clients at least once per month. More is fine as long as it is not overdone.
- Network aggressively: It is necessary to meet others frequently. Attend regional and national events to be known within your local community.

Things to Remember about Referrals

- Referrals are linked to loyal customers; ensure they remain loyal by remaining in contact.

- Use the $25 \times 30 \times 50$ method to remain in touch with customers monthly.
- Always ask for more than one referral; it builds up your future base quicker.
- Ask for referrals at the peak of the sale, not at the end. Do not leave time for dissonance.
- Referrals nurture value. Ensure customers understand your provided value.
- Use traditional and nontraditional methods to remain in contact with customers.
- Build community or join one so that others understand and can articulate your intended value.
- Create a value proposition so that customers become marketing avatars.
- Never stop asking for referrals; it is an endless process.

A quick word before you read the next chapter. Selling today requires that you make as many relationships as possible. Therefore, selling to a certain extent is very similar to marketing, whereby marketing is meant to establish relationships so that others can understand the value that you have. In Chapter 7, I will illustrate how you can utilize certain marketing techniques so that you can articulate the value and differentiate your potential database so that they become more attractive with less labor. I've discussed in previous chapters about value propositions and activities to help create those relationships and that's what the next chapter is all about.

CHAPTER 7

Wow It's Noisy—How to Get Heard in a Rock Concert

During his prime, rock legend Elton John was constantly castigated for the type of costumes he wore onstage in the 1970s. In our time, the latest rock legend Lady Gaga also seems to create levels of controversy with her styles of dress. However, what is most notable is that both seek to be contrary to the "same ole same ole."

When marketing, you need to do something that's completely different than anybody else. Marketing is similar to being at a rock concert—it's not about screaming louder, it's about looking different so that the singer or star recognizes you.

Too many in marketing today sound just like their competitor. There is no distinction and nothing that separates them from the competitor. Unless you're sounding differently or doing something differently no one will notice. You need to be like Elton John or Lady Gaga to be noticeable. This means that you must create promotional activities that enable awareness. It also requires you to being so noticeably different that others speak about you. This is the only way that marketing attraction can actually be built.

You might be thinking at this point what any of this has to do with selling? Well quite a lot in fact, what were looking to do is help you to create the relationships necessary so that people understand the value that you have. Over the years, I've seen too many sellers pick up the phone and begin a discussion with their stereotypical title and moreover the same ridiculous questions that every sales agent tends to ask. What I'm attempting to do here in this particular chapter is help you to stand head and shoulders or even above the competition so that you're able to conduct some type of attraction so that people come to you. My attitude and selling is that you need to become a potential customer magnet. It's too difficult in today's world to try to find all of the relationships necessary to help build your end of the practice. Therefore, my attempt in this particular chapter is to get people attracted to you so that you make more money and reduce your labor.

So What Do You Do That Is Different?

The way to avoid the trap of being just a regular selling professional and a high achiever is to refrain from the traditional model of features and benefits. Look at the client in terms of outcomes and results. No matter the issue, focus on how your organization provides the results the client seeks. It is not about facts, but the return on the client's investment.

Building your business is not about making money, but about creating the relationships and clients. The conversation with prospects should not be about features, but rather the value from you and your product or service. Do not focus on fees, commissions, costs, or any other sales-related words. If the discussion is not about value, then you have surrendered control of the discussion and the result will not be in your preferred terms. I recall a great quote from a mentor, Alan Weiss Seminar,

> Language controls discussion, discussion controls the relationship, and relationship controls the business.

When the conversation focuses on value, the prospect becomes convinced of the knowledge you provide and desires a relationship with you. Therefore, all discussions must focus on how working with your organization produces returns for the client with investment in time and money.

At this particular point in time, you might be asking yourself what is this value that I keep talking about. Value is nothing more than what the client is going to receive from conducting business with you. One might call it a benefit or in impractical terms, one might say that it's the return on investment from conducting business with you. I have found over my 32-year tenure in sales that too many people are transactional and only looking for a quick commission catch. Clients do not want us; they want a trusting relationship with someone they can continually return to. If you are not returning value then they will not return to you. Therefore, anything you do to help separate yourself from the pack is to always discuss with the clients how they will benefit from conducting business with you.

Utilizing this approach also requires that you become more proactive in your daily activities. In order to market like a rock star and be heard among the noisy competition, you must continually be looking out for your client. You should be researching competitive information, constantly become attuned to current events and news-related information in the industry. And, you should be presenting competitive positioning and industry-related facts that perhaps your client isn't aware of. Becoming more of a consultant will make you a better asset to the client and allow you to become a trusting colleague. As stated earlier, when they trust you, they want to build a relationship with you and moreover—continually conduct business with you.

Yet, positioning yourself to become a valuable asset not only requires you to be more consultative, but also requires you to alter who you are contacting. For many years during my keynotes, workshops, and seminars, I've always discussed with selling professionals that they must reach the key decision maker. This is more true now than ever! Selling professionals today by large are wasting too much time and too much energy interacting, engaging, and involving themselves with individuals who will not make a decision or purchase. I'm reminded of a former client by the name of Patrick, who was attempting to sell information technology managed services. He struggled for over two years and had sent out 55 proposals with no decisions and no sales. He was eventually terminated. The reason is that he wasted too much time and attention on individuals who were not entitled to make an acquisition.

The only person that a selling professional must speak with is the buyer! There are no ifs and buts to this simple statement. Selling professionals need not waste any time and any resources speaking with anyone other than the person who is willing to buy product from you and is ready to sign the check. Speaking with anyone else is simply a waste of time.

Finally, it's important to understand that buyers do not necessarily have titles or distinctive names. They will be hidden in departments of hierarchical organizations or have multiple responsibilities in small organizations. Therefore, it will become increasingly necessary for you to develop strategies as well as techniques to find the buyer of choice.

In just a moment, I am going to share with you a plethora of ways to be able to get your name in the mainstream so that you can become different from other selling professionals. You see, when you get your name into the marketplace and the mainstream, it becomes easier for buyers to find you. Therefore, when you actively participate in a multitude of ideas on a daily basis in order to find buyers, sometimes it is easier for buyers to find you when they have a need. So the list that I am about to share with you is actually going to decrease the need for cold calling, lead generation, and discovery by almost 75 percent!

Getting the Buyer to Find You

In order to find the buyer in an organization similar to the matter in which I introduced this chapter of Elton John or Lady Gaga, you must do it differently. Many of the following techniques you might've actually heard but it's important to review some of them again so that you can understand how to network aggressively, how to market yourself differently, and how to be distinctive in an exceedingly crowded marketplace. The following list of activities is not mutually exclusive. Sometimes, it is hard to use all instruments simultaneously. In fact, sometimes it is difficult to do so. That said, choose those who are congruent with your interests and those who can appeal instantly to your clients. Most importantly, what you need to be thinking of is that you're taking on one-to-many approach. What this means that you're not using the telephone, or conducting a tremendous amount of phone calls in order to meet one person. The idea here is to extend your reach by networking in front of a large group of individuals so that they get an idea of the value and differentiation you bring to the marketplace. I have a group of people in one room getting to know you in a relationship-oriented fashion and not a transaction will make you exceedingly popular and get people attracted by the manner in which you articulate your service offerings.

In the marketing world, this is typically called channel distribution or marketing promotion. In the sales world, it's getting your butt in front of as many people as possible. No matter what you want to call, it's actually the way to have the easiest access to a market that will be immediately interested in the things that you have to say and the implications in which you can help them. Here is just one of many items that you might be able to offer to extend your reach to the marketplace. There are more and I can make additional suggestions if you want by simply e-mailing me at Drew@Drew-Stevens.com

1. Speaking. One of the best methods to introduce your expertise is to tell others about what you do. Rotary's, Kiwanis, Chambers of Commerce are constantly in need of experts. Contact these practices or others to discuss content to enlighten their members. Participants are attracted by new and interesting content. There is a reason why Steve Jobs and Bill Gates are chronic keynote speakers and their brands continually manifest. You might speak at a local ladies auxiliary or a youth fitness class. Choose avenues where your clients will be.

2. Writing articles. There are more newspapers in circulation today then ever before. There is a multitude of newsletters, websites, regional business magazines, and local newspapers starving for decent material. Articles need not be more than 500 to 1,000 words. With good content and a solid byline, your message can be in the hands of hundreds or thousands. All individuals have something to offer and periodicals are always searching for content. Every sales professional is an expert in his or her respective business.

3. Website. The proliferation of the Internet allows others to discover your content and determine your value. Fees are inconsequential and the business world requires a website to denote your sincerity to clients. With over 300 million websites today, there is a need to be with the competition and clients expect you to have one. Clients research you before they call or contact. In fact, research for this area illustrates that Google searches top over 4.7 billion in any particular week. The Internet today is yesterday's Yellow Pages. Many

organizations, especially the one that you work for most probably has a website and there is no reason for your name and your value cannot be emblazoned on a page of the website.

4. Blogs. Similar to articles, having a blog serves two purposes: (1) remaining in constant contact with current subscribers and (2) enabling you to reach new clients at relatively no cost. The difference from articles is immediacy of availability and frequency of your content. Procter & Gamble has a blog, its penetration helps to reach over 1 million people daily, and the feedback has been successful in creating new products and services. Blogs allow you to provide your expertise in a particular area and get your knowledge out in the market to those that seek it. And it is a great way for you to maintain relationships with your clients. This is especially valuable if you want to provide updates on product and service offerings, say in a podcast or even in a good cast. Most importantly, it will separate you from the remainder of transactional nod heads and competitors, who call themselves selling professionals.

5. Lunch and learns. These concise information sessions last no longer than 30 minutes during a corporate luncheon and feature your content. Benefits are a live audience, interested attendees, and low cost of acquisition. The intent is not only delivery, but also possible business from attendees. Many fitness professionals, insurance, and service practices use these successful ventures. Research companies around your region that would be interested in gaining some insight into health, wellness, and other areas of corrective health. Have them bring a sack lunch and you speak for a short time on some health topic of interest to them.

6. Booklets. Typically focused on one topic, these small content-rich pieces feature your advice on one particular topic, that is, nutrition. Booklets can be used for potential clients as handouts or products to be sold at special events. Booklets are low cost and can be produced at a local printer. These take just a few moments to develop and provide tremendous free value. You might decide to work with your marketing team and develop a small booklet of 6 to 10 pages related to a feature or cool offering about your product and service.

7. Networking. Chambers and associations exist for a valid reason. When others become aware of your service and if using your value proposition, they desire more information. Recall individuals who conduct business with those they know and trust. Local communities are tremendous ways and build quick relationships. Never ever avoid the power of the network.

8. Cause marketing. With the increased focus on ethics and social responsibility, many practices give back to the community while teaming with nonprofit organizations. "Teaming" with practice that seeks similar goals as yours alleviates marketing costs. One of the best cause marketing campaigns is the Susan G. Komen practice. Beginning in the early 1990s, this nonprofit organization collaborated with numerous corporate entities and became the preeminent donor of breast cancer awareness.

9. Trade shows. Trade associations and exhibition are terrific methods to express brand. Trade shows require effort and focus, and a myriad of issues can fail if the show is not conducted properly. However, these exhibitions are great methods for meeting new clients, and maintaining contact with existing ones. However, do not enter a trade show without a proper game plan and key performance indicators.

10. Pro bono work. What committees can you work on or what associations do you know of in need of your passions and talents? This type of work gets you very involved in your community and creates the visibility required for potential clients. Other than time, there is minimal expense and much return on investment.

11. Referrals. The sweetest sound any sales professional can hear are the encouraging words from existing clients who know and appreciate your value. When they tell others your advertising is lower and more become attracted to you. And when requested in multiples, there is never a need to advertise and promote again since your current base informs the world of your great results!

12. Newsletters. Printed monthly or quarterly and sent to existing and possibly prospective clients, this information-packed value must be easy to read and full of great tactics clients can instantly use. Provide

good intellectual property so that people become interested in waiting for the next edition.

13. Teaching. Education is everywhere. From online to community centers association and universities are constantly seeking subject matter experts to present data to students. Teaching allows you to manifest your brand, get you in front of an audience of potential clients, and allows you the opportunity to research information for future hourly presentations. I am reminded of the time when I walked into a classroom three years after having met a former student. I was about to begin class and Jennifer called me up on the telephone saying I need to hire you for a keynote event that we are doing in June please put June 5 on your calendar. For five minutes worth of work I received an $80,000 contract.

14. Alliances. There are many people who honor and believe in sales professional, but you may not have met them. This includes anyone from medical practitioners to physical therapists, coaches, and beauticians, even attorneys that handle personal injury. Take the time to meet as many as possible to help grow your brand above and beyond your own capabilities.

15. Sponsorships. Different from advertising and passive listings such as directories and Yellow Pages, sponsorships get your brand in front of very targeted audiences such as runners, bikers, cancer survivors, and so on. Find organizations that can appreciate and help you get your name in front of those that need it.

The market today requires you to be visible, that is, how people know of you and use your services. When you are invisible you are ghostly and hidden. When you use the power of integrated marketing communications you create duplicity of channels to manifest your brand. Exploit as many channels as possible to grow your brand, create noise, and attract future markets to you.

Getting Rid of Stereotype

I work with many business owners and selling professionals. When I ask them what they do they immediately rush into their title. Each states,

"I am the President of a Bank," "I am a Consultant," "and I am a Professional Speaker." If I were a client and heard this, I would have immediately stated, "So What"? Professionals today refrain from their titles and occupations in the service business and speak with the reply to "So What"? The method for doing so is known as a "value proposition."

Simply put, a value proposition is a pithy statement that promotes the business to clients using outcome and results. This brief statement denotes the benefit(s) that a client receives from working with you. It is outcome based and focuses all attention on client outcomes not process, method, or anything further.

Research for this book with over 7,500 sales professionals illustrates that many firms (93 percent) focus on process and not client outcomes. Exemplars include:

- We provide sales training.
- Our assessments assist with personality profiling.
- We analyze your issues with a needs assessment.
- Our model incorporates organizational redesign and leadership development.

These are not value propositions. While they indicate information about the organization, they do nothing else but focus on the organization. The entire purpose of a value proposition is to focus on sole benefit to the client.

The proliferation of both the Internet and small business has created a conundrum of noise and activity around clients. That said, it is vital for your services to be heard. Organizations today require focus on two complicated issues: productivity and profitability—your mission is to create a succinct message that addresses these concerns to the decision maker.

Be mindful, this is not an elevator speech. The value proposition succinctly addresses the concern. Dependent on the offered results, the statement might also help with brand! A perfect example is FedEx—absolutely guaranteed to be there overnight. Not only is this one of the most powerful value propositions in the world, but also one of the best brands.

There are other reasons for writing a value proposition:

- Distinguishes you from the competition.
- Distinguishes you and the organization in distinctive markets.
- Provides a better source of lead generation.
- Accomplishes quicker time to market.
- Enables selling professionals to expediently get in front of decision makers.

This tool contains no more than 10 to 15 words featuring as many adjectives as possible. Value propositions have these characteristics:

- Focus on what the buyer gets, it is outcome based.
- Results focused that uses colorful words to gain the attention.
- General in that the statement can appeal to any industry dependent on need.

Here is an example to develop a value proposition:

1. *A poor value proposition*:
   - We help create a fit individual
2. *A good value proposition*:
   - We have a seven-step program for better abdominals
3. *A great value proposition*:
   - We dramatically accelerate results that match your individual fitness desires

The concept for developing a statement is not difficult to achieve, yet it takes a lot of patience. It is vital to look at the organization from a customer or competitive point of view.

Questions to answer are:

1. What does your organization do that from a benefit and results perspective stands head and shoulders above any competitive pressure?

2. What results do clients achieve with you?
3. What is the organization extremely passionate for in meeting client's needs?
4. What are your core values that provide results to clients?
5. What an individual or organizational values, provide value to clients?
6. How does the organization minimize client risk and provide a return on investment?

These are only a few of the many questions that can be asked to begin crafting a message. Do not expect to obtain a statement overnight yet do not belabor it either. Too many organizations spend countless hours on mission, vision, and values, yet the organizational culture does not exemplify the creed or shamefully do not understand it. However, if you desire better results for your sales and marketing efforts, it is best to begin with asking questions focused on client value and return on investment—to the client. If you cannot gain the answers, the best source is your clients! Testimonials and case studies are great examples of value. Take their statements and simply develop them into benefit-based sentences.

It is imperative to understand that no magic formula exists for the creation of a value proposition. Further, it is an often overlooked and underutilized tool. And, organizations typically confuse mission and vision statements with these benefit-based phrases. However, when researched, reviewed, and required, these thought-provoking statements might assist your organization to break away from the pack. The drafting of an articulate message might be split second differentiator between a cursory review of your competitor's brochure or phone call and yours. Craft a new message, speak of value and results, and watch the gap widen.

There are two skills needed to leverage the power of a value proposition for landing pages:

1. You need to be able to *identify* an effective value proposition.
2. You need to be able to *express* an effective value proposition as well as have others express it too.

Answer the following questions specifically but succinctly:

1. What is unique about the brand and your offering? Write this down. In addition, write down the first thing that comes to mind when others want to know what you do. However, return to the previous sections to help develop statements based on customer needs and perceived value.

2. What do you do that is different from competitors? Write it down as succinctly as possible. Use adjectives and adverbs when possible.

3. What is the *best choice* for your optimum customer? What is the output or results to the client? How is the clients' repute improved? Look at the master list of words in the appendix, what words can you incorporate into your current value sentence.
   Examples include:
   - Dramatic
   - Accelerate
   - Speed to Market
   - Expediency
   - Proficiency
   - Compliant

4. Rewrite your first statement with the use of differentiation and optimum value to the client. Review and develop a value sentence that eschews facts and provides output and results to the reader/listener. Use adjectives and adverbs that profess the deliverables to the client. *Do not worry about word count or language at this juncture.*

5. Ask yourself: If you had just 10 to 20 words with which to describe why people should buy from your company instead of someone else, what would you communicate? Looking at your sentence in question four, can you rephrase/rewrite your sentence in 20 words or less using some of the word choices above?

Plan your draft here:

_____

_____

_____

Write a second draft

_____

_____

_____

Final Thoughts on Being Heard among the Noise

This chapter is focused intently on numerous marketing aspects that can be used so that you are heard among the competition. And, one of the chapters of this book provides some focus on overall aspects of customer service. However, I do want to offer some final guidelines to assist you so that you provide more value to your clients and illustrate some disruption in the highly competitive profession. Yes, sales is an exceedingly competitive profession and the more disruption you provide the more opportunities will present themselves to you.

One of the first things that I typically notice with selling professionals or organizations that hire sales professionals is that they continually utilize transactional techniques that get no results. On any one typical business, I get no less than five cold calls from individuals who are more transactional than relational. Selling is a relationship-oriented business and no one is going to buy products or services from anyone "pitching products" that also has to make over 50 calls per day. If you want to be disruptive then it is best to research your client, gain referrals, and determine ways of directly networking with people who could make decisions of your products and services rather than calling them on the phone and interrupting their day.

Additionally, if you are attempting to reach an individual whom you've not met and would like access to then it is best to draft a personal letter that indicates not necessarily why you are attempting to reach them but rather positions you and your services in offering a competitive situation. When you position from a competitive prospective what your products or services have done for other competitive companies you illustrate your value. Further, providing an action step such as "I will call you on Friday at 10 a.m. to discuss this letter and an opportunity to meet with you" illustrates your professionalism and desire for relationship rather than just calling to "pitch your product" and appear transactional.

Third, another disruptive method of reaching buyers is using handwritten letters or even sending your letters via Federal Express or United Parcel Service. There are too many individuals who become lackadaisical due to the availability of e-mail and instant messaging. I myself was recently involved with purchasing a car but never spoke to the sales representative because he never picked up the phone! He repeatedly text messaged me rather than build a relationship. Needless to say he did not get the business. If you're seeking to be heard then do the things that make you more visible in the eyes of the customer. Handwritten letters and note cards, personal phone calls, and even direct interfaces make you more valuable than your competitor.

Fourth, ensure that you utilize voicemail in the best way possible. Provide a very professional message that indicates your concern for hearing the message, your desire for returning calls quickly, and resolving the person's question. For example, my voicemail message clearly indicates that I return all calls within 90 minutes. People love it and constantly challenge me to return calls in 89 minutes! However, aside from the banter, the message is clear; my concern is to respond to the client more efficiently and effectively than my competitor.

Finally, while there has been talk here about professional nuances there is one other that is just as important as every other ideology discussed. If you really want to be disruptive and stand out among the competition then you need to dress different from the competition. I recently conducted a workshop for commercial mortgage brokers, who had the opportunity to make over $1 million a year. During the workshop, I was indicating certain things such as having a good pen. I was questioned whether or not someone signing a $15 million loan would be concerned over the type of pen in your hand. My response—yes! If you want to be disruptive then you need to dress the part. Many firms today have opted for the business casual experience and this is not in the best interest of customer relations. Selling is a profession similar to medical, legal, and financial services. If you want to gain the respect, the courtesy, and more importantly the financial reward from conducting business with someone else, then you must dress better and smarter than the person on the other side of the desk. My recommendation is to have a good expensive pair of shoes, a business suit, a leather portfolio or padfolio, a handcrafted business card holder, and an expensive pen. I am not endorsing any one particular product, but dressing for success will not only create more success for you to make you feel better simultaneously.

It's an extremely crowded marketplace and the one which requires your attention to not only being opportunistic, but also disruptive. The profession of selling has become more competitive because of the need to sell products and services to the numerous demographics that have entered the markets. Moreover, consumers have too many choices among competitors and the Internet has created disintermediation between vendor and consumer. In certain circles, sales professionals become more of a commodity. With so many challenges and so many consumers, it is time for selling professionals to make the necessary changes so that they can rise like a Phoenix.

Best Practices and Action Steps

- Review the aforesaid list and make a chart or table that provides at least four to five activities that you will conduct weekly. Begin to chart your progress to illustrate how many new people you're meeting on a weekly basis to help extend your reach.
- Contact at least one local newspaper or radio station to determine if you can write an article or provide industry insight to the media or commentary on local business ideas.
- Use the worksheet provided to you in this chapter to help create an articulate value proposition. Don't worry about perfection, but begin utilizing the proposition when you're networking with individuals. For example, if you're meeting a new individual and they ask what you do just don't tell them that you're an account manager for XYZ Association. With your new value proposition, indicate to them that you create relationships that enforce better financial decisions. You might be selling accounting services or be a financial analyst, but you

need not use the stereotype to indicate the value you provide the potential buyers.

- Review some of the companies that you would like to access company buyers. Align those types of buyers with particular activities mentioned earlier in this chapter to determine how to attract them to you. For example, if some of these read a regional newspaper or even a national magazine you might want to see whether you can write an article.
- Create a blog or website that illustrates your expertise in the market. Utilize very clear search engine optimization tactics so that when others are seeking people with your experience, you will be clearly illustrated in a simple Internet search.

Just a word before we go to the next chapter. We discussed some of the ways in which individuals can become attracted to you. However, one of the most important people that need to be attracted are those that are buyers. Too many selling professionals today get subordinated to others that don't make decisions. The only methodology that will make you a truly successful salesperson in today's competitive world is by becoming one-on-one with the economic buyer. Therefore, I'm going to help you in the next chapter by illustrating methods for you to become a buyer, so that you meet more people who will buy from you and help to eliminate all of the gaps in the sales process. So let's read on, I'll meet you on the next page.

CHAPTER 8

Becoming a Buyer Peer

I'm going to utilize a classic Dale Carnegie opening question on you. "If there were a way that I can reduce your labor and create higher levels of selling success would you be interested"? Of course you would say yes! What I have found in over 30 years of selling is that too many individuals spend time with subordinates and not enough with buyers. I truly mean the individuals who can make a decision, write a check, and say yes to you. When you meet buyers, you immediately eliminate all the obstacles in the sales process and actually lessen the sales process. There are too many selling professionals today meeting individuals who are simply wasting their time and never able to make a decision. And, they're found in every level of every hierarchical organization.

In the previous chapters, I illustrated to you ways in which people can become attracted to you. I wrote a significant amount about this so that they were byways for both subordinates as well as buyers to find you. Whether you have people coming to you or you need to find business, your focal point should always be on the economic buyer—the person who signs the check and makes the decision. This particular chapter is established solely so that you find that one individual who will help eliminate all of the negation and all of the bureaucracy so that he or she gets the value and you get the win!

This book has discussed a number of techniques for being different among the crowd, but none is more important than establishing a relationship so that you and the buyer are equals. This is important because any other relationship makes you nothing more than a vendor to the buying organization. When this occurs, you not only subordinate position to the buyer, but also to the entire relationship. If you don't think that's true then it will be interesting to see how you respond to the following set of questions:

1. Have you on more than one occasion had your meeting canceled with whom you believe to be the buyer?
2. During your meeting with the buyer, have they placed someone else in charge?
3. Are you told that future meetings and conversations need to be held with XXXXX?

If you have had specific answers to these questions then your position has been subordinated and you are not a buyer peer. When you are a peer of the buyer they look up to you for advisory services and think of you as a colleague who is there to help them with competitive positioning or even a revenue problem. The peers look at each other as equals and not as transactional vendors. So the remainder of the time here will be spent assisting you with becoming a peer of the buyer.

First and foremost, if you want to be a peer of the buyer you need to act like one. Age and experience do not matter to a potential buyer, especially if you're offering a method that can help achieve productivity and profitability. Every good buyer in existence today is seeking just that. This does not denote that your characteristics change, that you become a narcissist, or that you act cocky. It simply means that you will have no fear in speaking with somebody who can make a decision, no matter the age, the gender, the culture, or the amount of professional experience. When you "walk the walk and talk the talk," people will respect you more.

Second, you absolutely must be prepared when deciding to meet a buyer. It is imperative that you utilize services such as Google or Reuters or Bloomberg to understand current company information, the company's history, its strategy, and most importantly the industry and the competition. Once you have conducted your homework, it is then necessary for you to position your products or services in a way to help the potential buyer. In other words, what does your product or service do that will help enhance the firm's competitive position. For example, if you're an advertising agency, have you worked on campaigns that have broadened the brand and increase the value to its demographic base? Or, if you are a manufacturer or distributor of certain food items, do you have access to less expensive foods or even regional access that not only helps with the firm's expenses but also makes it socially responsible? The more you can position your products and services in terms of outcomes and success factors for the prospective buyer, the easier it will be to become a peer.

Third, great salespeople who want to be buyer peers know how to listen more. This means that selling professionals visit with the buyer with a well-prepared dossier of provocative questions that they want to ask the buyer. These are questions but hope engage buyers into good discussion and open dialogue. Further, they're not the rote questions asked by most selling professionals. These include, but are not limited to, "so when are you looking to make an acquisition" or "if your boss were in the room what might he or she say." Such questions come out of sales books and magazines from the 1980s and do little to build a relationship. You must have great questions prepared that get the customer to think and respond in a challenging way.

Fourth, it's been discussed earlier in this book but suffice to say you need to offer to the potential buyer the value that you're providing. Therefore, anything that you say must correspond to outcomes the buyer will gain from doing business with you. Think in terms of the amount of wins a buyer gains when doing business with you.

Language of the Sale

Many years ago, I had an opportunity to work with the management guru Alan Weiss. He has a philosophy that states that all conversations with buyers must have good discussion. In other words, when selling professionals are initially meeting with prospective buyers and engaging in conversation then they must speak. In other words, prospective buyers are always thinking about the strategic orientation of the organization, meeting goals and objectives of the organization, and how to keep the organization productive and profitable. Therefore, all conversations must conform to having good discussion so that the buyer is always engaged with understanding how you can assist.

One of the best ways of understanding developer relationship with the buyer is shown in Figure 8.1.

If one would look at developing a relationship with the buyer from start to finish, it might look something like mentioned in Figure 8.1. In order to develop the initial conversation, you must know where the buyer goes. And, the conversation has to be more than simply a hello and let's

Initial conversation Exchange Determine Understand Relationship Agreement Proposal Implementation New
business   value   KPIs   returns

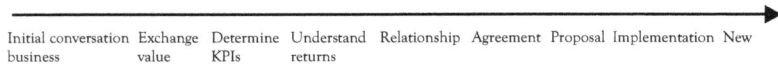

Figure 8.1 The Conversation Flov

get together for lunch. There has to be a valid reason for requesting an initial conversation with the buyer. I am reminded of a very old movie starring the actress Melanie Griffith entitled "Working Girl." Without going into the full synopsis of the script, Ms. Griffith is attempting to meet to set up a merger for a very high profile CEO of a corporate firm to expand into radio so that it increases its portfolio and gain more profitability. When she gets with the CEO of the firm—Oren Trask, she does not merely butter him up with pleasantries, but rather expresses the desire to meet so that Trask Industries increases its portfolio in a very competitive industry—he naturally agrees. As you can see, Ms. Griffith enacts as a salesperson in order to establish value so that she brings the relationship to the next level.

Once the initial conversation is established in value exchanged now, it is time to understand some of the most important pieces said that the salesperson can bring the relationship to the next level. he utilizes a model known as OMV—Objectives—Measures and Values. It is a rather simple model but one that invokes the trustworthiness of the relationship and propels it to a level sought after by most economic buyers. OMV simply stands for objectives, measures, and values. Every good decision maker requires these three ideals because he or she is simply looking at returns on investment. When you establish a conversation that includes objectives, measurements, and values, the buyer will listen while stating to himself or herself "this sales person understands my concerns and how to aid me in a consultative manner." OMV illustrates that you have conducted your homework and are willing to conduct the relationship on the buyers level not yours—not transactional but relationship oriented, and most importantly, different from your competitors. In the next few paragraphs, I want to help you understand what objectives, measures, and values are.

Goals and Objectives

It is quite easy to say that objectives are nothing more than what the buyer is looking to accomplish. Buyers are simply looking for methods that can help them achieve answers to many of the issues that plagued them on a day-to-day basis. Most high-level buyers are always concerned about productivity and profitability. They seek methods for decreasing costs and achieving the highest levels of productivity for either the department or the entire organization. Therefore, if you're meeting with the buyer, you simply need to establish what his or her objectives are as soon as possible. To help you establish a methodology with understanding objectives, here are some questions to help you get started:

- What is the ideal outcome you'd like to experience?
- What results are you trying to accomplish?
- What better product/service/customer condition are you seeking?
- Why are you seeking to do this (work/project/engagement)?
- Are shareholders pushing you in a certain direction?
- What results is the Board of Directors seeking for you to gain?
- What ideas do you have on the table today for increasing profitability and productivity?
- What are some factors you would like to see to become more expeditious to market?

I would suggest that once you have established a meeting with the buyer, you create a list of questions based upon some levels of research conducted. For example, if you have read the annual report, current news, and conducted some levels of business intelligence about the industry, the competition, and the company itself, then I would suggest to develop a list of questions to ask the potential buyer; these questions may vary for different organizations or buyers, but you do need a set of questions to ask on each and every call.

Returns Required—Key Performance Evaluators

Once you have established a set of questions for your objectives then you will need a list of questions to understand the measurements for that buyer to visually understand the success that you and your organization can bring. Measurements are simply that they are the key performance indicators that help the buyer understand whether or not your product or service can achieve the results they desire.

For a key performance indicator to work, a key performance indicator must be based on legitimate data and provide context that echoes business objectives. They must be defined in a way that factors beyond the control of a company cannot interfere with their fulfillment. Another key factor is that they have specific time frames divided into key checkpoints. So when we review the characteristics of a measurement, we are seeking to review issues surrounding the following areas:

- Quantitative: They can be presented in form of numbers.
- Practical: They integrate well with present company processes.
- Directional: They help to determine if a company is getting better.
- Actionable: They can be put into practice to effect desired change.

There is no specific number of Key Performance Indicators (KPIs) a company needs. In general, the number may be anywhere from four to ten for many types of businesses, and they must be crucial to the success of the business. Nothing is important if everything is important, the ideology here is not to necessarily help develop the key performance metric that the buyers are seeking, but merely to understand how they're going to measure the success in acquiring your product or service. By working with them, your relationship may actually help to develop a KPI not already in existence. Yet, it's important for you to ask the right questions so that you understand not only what the buyer wants, but also the fact that the buyer has made the right decision to acquire your product. Understand making the right decision, and helping them to make that decision will help to eliminate buyer's remorse. Here are some questions you might want to ask:

- How will you know we've accomplished your intent?
- What indicators will you use to assess our progress?
- Each time we talk, what standard will tell us we're progressing?
- How would you know it if you tripped over it?
- Is there a particular time frame that you're seeking?

- Is there a particular trend you're seeking?
- What percentage or margin of error are you looking to increase or decrease?

Benefits of Conducting Business with You

Once you have completed your line of questioning related to the measurements in order to achieve success, it is now time for you to focus on the value that you will bring to the organization. There are many times that the buyer may not be able to articulate the value that they are seeking. Sometimes it's visual, sometimes it's implied, and sometimes it's unknown.

Your job as a selling professional is to help them uncover what that value is. There are many times that I simply asked the question how would you know that we have delivered the value if you tripped over it? I cannot help them if they cannot help me understand what it is that they're looking to achieve. I recall a time when I was speaking with Tina, who is with a very large travel organization that was seeking some remedies for her sales team. After approximately 20 to 30 minutes of asking her the right questions, she was finally able to articulate that what she was really seeking was to stop the lethargy in the sales pipeline. Sometimes all you need to do is ask the right questions in the right order and in such a way that helps the buyer communicate what exactly they seek. Here are some of the questions that you might want to ask:

- How would you assess the actual return (Return on Investments, Return on Assets, Return on Sales, Return on Equity, etc.)?
- What would be the extent of the improvement (or correction)?
- How will these results impact the bottom line?
- What are the annualized savings (first year might be deceptive)?
- What is the intangible impact (e.g., on repute, safety, comfort, etc.)?
- How would you, personally, be better off or better supported?

And now that you've asked a series of questions to help get the relationship on the conversation started, you are now able to move the conversation forward with helping the client to understand your product and service offerings and how you can assist them. This is not to say that you would go into a complete product demonstration; however, you might, for example, want to set up a separate meeting to do this or you might be ready to move the conversation to the next level. In some cases, this might be a proposal, a purchase order, or simply a yes. What I am suggesting here is moving the conversation to the level but it needs to go to in order to obtain agreement so that you can close the sale. It is what many sales mentors and pundits would call agreement.

This is where I believe most selling professionals get trumped. Many selling professionals get very excited because they've had a conversation with the client. The sales professionals believe they can move the conversation to the next level—in most cases, they believe this is the proposal phase. This is not necessarily true! First, the selling professionals must meet with the true buyer. If the buyer cannot write a check or force someone to make a check then they are not a buyer. Moreover, if after meeting someone you have been subordinated to another person or even another person at a lower level, then you do not have a peer relationship. The person that you would have met with believed you to be no more than a vendor. The only way in which you can move the conversation in the relationship to the next level is ensuring you have had a provocative conversation with someone that is decisive and who then signs a contract based upon your value.

Second, assuming for a moment you have met with someone who can actually sign the check for you, then the conversation centered around objectives, measurements, and values will assist you with understanding whether or not you're ready to negotiate business. The reason for this is because once you have gotten some type of understanding of the objectives, measurements, and values and the buyer is aware of how you and your services might help the firm, they may simply ask you for something in writing to help cement the conversation. The next step is a simple letter agreement based upon the conversation.

In most sales inner circles, this is known as the proposal. However, the proposal is probably the most misunderstood document. Proposals are nothing more than a written reiteration of your conversation with the buyer. They are not meant to add anything other than an investment estimate. Therefore, a buyer should never be surprised by any content seen in a proposal. Most importantly, proposals should be succinct. There is no reason other than certain industries that require templates to be followed (and I don't normally get involved with firms that demand; I send a proposal without meeting with the buyer) that your proposal should be no more than two to five pages. In certain instances, it might go a bit further but it does not have to be the next nonfiction novel.

This correlates with the treatment that you should have with someone who could buy your services. Your concern for brevity is imperative to a buyer who has little time and attention. Additionally, by being brief you illustrate that you are an equal of the buyer. As you are probably well aware that selling professionals always have to talk. By being brief, you're disrupting the sales training by illustrating your confidence to the buyer.

Being one with the buyer is an important concept and one that requires an incomparable amount of self-esteem. You've got to have the confidence to be with individuals who are making important daily decisions. You also have to be confident enough that they are neither smarter nor better than you—they are merely different. And, you also need to take risks and be bold with a buyer similar in which they are with you. Do not be pushed around by someone who can make a decision. You can push back and by doing so you illustrate your equality with the buyer, after all, they are merely people too. I would suggest reviewing this chapter on a periodic basis so that you are as comfortable as possible when initiating conversations with buyers. I also suggest that you extol your limited beliefs in thinking there are certain individuals better than you. The more confident you are and the more comfortable you are in meeting individuals who can write you a check, the more successful you will be in selling yourself and your organization's products and services.

Best Practices and Action Steps

- Attend a networking event solicited solely by the economic buyer you're trying to find.
- Establish a proper list of questions and predispositions based upon the buyer's need.
- Create a list of questions based upon objectives that particular economic buyer is attempting to reach.

- Conduct an online search or get assistance from a regional library to conduct a deep analysis on the company you're attempting to reach and the buyer you want to gain access to. You must build an account management profile, which illustrates the lines of business, the industry, the competition, and the value you bring to the organization.
- Create a list of objections you might hear from a buyer and develop peer methods to defend your position.
- Practice in the mirror or with a friend when a buyer attempts to believe you so that you can push back in a more comfortable way while doing so.

Just a few words before moving to the next chapter. Dealing with buyers is going to be quite difficult. You have to have a tremendous amount of confidence and conviction in what you do. One of the things I've learned over 30 years of selling is not to worry about unsolicited feedback and to understand that I am in control of what happens. I know that anybody control the outcome, it's completely up to me. I understand that attempting to meet buyers and making these calls to meet people is quite difficult, but it does require a certain aptitude and behavior so that you're comfortable in your own shoes. I typically would not write about this in a sales but I believe today's seller is quite different. Today's contemporary selling professional needs to have a certain air of confidence and cockiness so that they can rise above all of the competitive pressures. By that I mean they have to be a master in self-awareness and self-gratification. So to help you understand the process and how to gain more confidence in what you're doing, I'm providing the following chapter on self-mastery so that you can understand some of the principles and feel better about what you do on a daily basis. Those who feel better about themselves will be able achieve more than those who lack confidence.

CHAPTER 9

Sales Tools for Today's Seller

When you look at any carpenter they typically have tools around their toolbelt. Before surgery, any sales professional reviews the tray for all of the surgical tools before performing the recommended operation. And, any musician such as a guitarist or pianist will always have something to tune his or her instrument prior to playing. In a similar fashion, a selling professional must have the proper tools in order to perform his or her work. Without the proper resources, it is impossible for any selling professional to conduct the necessary research to find buyers and it will be impossible to contact them without proper technology tools.

I recall having started in sales around 30 years ago; the only thing I had at my disposal was a telephone, a pen or pencil, and something called a Rolodex. Beyond that not much was available. Presently, the proliferation of both computer-assisted technology and the Internet has created an abundance of resources for sales professionals. These include, but are not limited to, databases, meeting conference tools, tools to help customers with testimonials and case studies, and even telephony tools that enable both buyer and seller to speak wherever and whenever possible.

It is wonderful to be able to talk about value and it's also wonderful to have the confidence to talk about that value. However, the most important item for any and every selling professional today is having the proper resources so that they can conduct the myriad of conversations required daily. You would not expect an automobile mechanic to repair your car without the proper tools. Well, no selling professional can approach a key economic buyer or even an influencer without having the proper tools to do so. Additionally, selling professionals must also have the proper tools so that they can conduct themselves in the most professional manner possible all navigating through the maze of bureaucracy, hierarchy, and monotony that creates the sales process. This chapter is about gaining access to the proper resources so that you save time and energy, and eliminate frustration.

The First Step Is Research

When conducting workshops and consulting, I advocate that before a selling professional picks up a telephone and says hello, he or she must have information on whom they are calling. Sales intelligence requires the use of industry information and proper research to understand information on the company, its chief competitors, and the industry. It is vital for the seller to understand the products and services of the prospective business. A review of current customers and issues affecting the company are useful since the content can be used to drive discussion with the economic buyer. Another interesting perspective is that sellers are outsiders and they see trends and threats that customers might not. Using the information as a method to show the customer what they do not see is very effective.

The most bountiful sources of company information come directly from annual reports, national newspapers, and even the Internet. A simple Google search helps those searching for client information with a wealth of content. There also exist a myriad of company databases such as Hoover's, Sorkin's, InfoUSA, and Leadership Directories that offer content-rich profiles.

For anyone selling today, especially when attempting to conduct business-to-business sales, it is imperative for every representative to research the company website and not only review products and services, but also the company's annual report. Every publicly traded company in the world must have an annual report available for investors as demanded by the Securities and Exchange Commission. However, the annual report serves as a tremendous resource for vendors, suppliers, and sales professionals, who desire to understand important financial information as well as the company position. I always have sales professionals', the CEOs', or presidents' message at the beginning of the annual report because it always provides tremendous amount of information on the financial stature, competitiveness, and innovations of the organization. It is from here that a research-oriented sales professional can then begin to develop the necessary value in order to approach the buyer. If you are not reviewing the annual report, you're missing out on a tremendous opportunity to present information in a way that the buyer will understand your value.

For privately held firms it becomes more challenging as most private institutions will not have an annual report. Therefore, the best places to review privately held information would be on the company's website and to conduct a simple Google search to understand if there is any new information. A simple search might produce enough information so that you can glean enough data in order to produce a value proposition for your organization.

When all else fails there are then databases. Organizations such as Hoover's, Sorkin's, InfoUSA, and Leadership Directories produce a wealth of information on organizations and executives. Please understand that I make no compensation for my recommendation on any of these products or services, but I have used them for years and believe in the value that they provide. All of these have produced not only a wealth of information, but also the backbone of financial success, that is why I highly recommend them. Please note that third-party companies produce most databases so a fee will always be associated for accessing information. However, there are some ways around having paid for many of these services. I highly recommend visiting your local library or university that will often have free accessibility. As an example for years, I have taught at several major universities and have continual access to their electronic libraries. Such electronic resources provide me with annual reports, historical information in terms of news, and the databases for accessing executive level biographies. If possible, I highly recommend that you visit with your local library and speak with a librarian to understand what is offered.

The two most valuable sources that I have used over the years are Hoover's and Leadership Directories. What I admire about Hoover's is the wealth of information they have. For example, there are over 80 million companies listed in their local databases that allow the user to develop lead generation reports, mailing lists, and even competitive information. Hoover's will list a short biography of the organization, the key players in the organization such as the CEO and the CFO, and the top competitors to that organization. This invaluable snapshot provides some of the important data necessary to begin your initial research. Most importantly, I like the feature that e-mails you any changes with executive personnel so that you can instantly develop new sales and marketing strategies.

Leadership Directories researches and provides profile and contact information for hundreds of thousands of decision makers and organizations in the United States. They provide products that feature in-depth individual and organization profiles of the U.S. Congress, federal government, state and local governments, public and private companies, law firms and courts, media outlets, health-care organizations, nonprofits, and associations that are available in print, online, mobile, and on demand. At last check they collect data for well over 700,000 businesses. I have always found this my most invaluable resource, especially when attempting to reach an economic buyer at the top echelons within a large enterprise. I will never forget attempting to reach the chief financial officer of Ernst & Young back in the early 1990s. I used Leadership Directories to review the company information and found that they listed every important officer including his telephone number, his facsimile number, and his executive assistant. Today, the data also include e-mails for both individuals and perhaps the most inviting resource of all is the ability to download such content into custom relational databases or even a simple spreadsheet. If you want to reach the top officer in the easiest fashion possible, then I truly believe the Leadership Directories is the proper resource.

Telephone

For many reading this book, talking about the need for a telephone may not seem too important, especially if you're working for a large business but if you are working virtually or for yourself and sales, a quick review of telephone equipment will be worthwhile. With many opting for less expensive telephony alternatives and many others attempting to completely utilize singular resources; the Internet allows for easy telephone connectivity. With that in mind, your telephone handset should have a good connection to it so that you can have uninterrupted conversations. It is also imperative that you have a hold button, a conference call button, and I also recommend the use of a very good headset. The latter allows your hands to be free so that you can take notes and listen more intently to the individual you're speaking with.

Business Card

You might believe that talking about a business card is rather naïve but in today's demographically altering world, business cards are different around the world. Here in the United States, we believe that a business card is just that, something that introduces you as a representative of an organization. However, globally and culturally business cards are actually called name cards and they are statement of purpose and value to the person holding it. Unfortunately, they are dismissed in the United States but exceedingly important around the globe. For example, here in the United States when conducting a meeting with most individuals they will take the business card of another and place it in their pocket. Globally, this is a sign of disrespect and most cards are held onto and face the reader with the proper surname so that the individual knows whom they're conversing with. To that end, I recommend having a business card with not only your American name and title, but also a translation on the other side dependent upon the global individuals you speak with. To exemplify my point, when I was working with many representatives of Japanese financial institutions, my business card had my American name and title on one side and on the reverse side the same information was written in Kanji and Katakana, the Japanese equivalent. Making such a cultural change makes you more proficient and more professional in the global setting.

There are many other tools that I can recommend to you and in most cases there are a few too many to name. Over the next several pages, I have developed a series of tools that will be exceedingly helpful for you in reducing your risk and making you a highly proficient selling representative. Again, I want to state that I make no compensation on the following recommendations. These tools have been vandalized by me for well over 31 years and I have found them most efficient and effective in not only operating my business, but also helping clients.

E-mail Communication

Aside from a telephone, one of the most important communication tools available today is e-mail. I remember the use of e-mail during the late 1980s: my goodness has it changed! Back then, we utilized terminals with green screens that had an 80 column by 24 line display without having the sexy graphical user interfaces that we have today! Clearly, e-mail today has altered so that we can quickly initiate a conversation with someone, reply to someone, and in certain cases (dependent upon the type of e-mail system you utilize or some of the possible tools that you can integrate), gain social media updates, news, or other important information about the particular subject. No matter what, e-mail makes it that much easier to correspond with prospective clients as well as provide an inordinate amount of customer support to retain clients.

During the many years of operation, I have used several different types of e-mail systems. These include, but are not limited to, names such as Eudora, CompuServe, AOL, and finally Microsoft Outlook. I recall when Microsoft introduced the Microsoft suite of products in the late 1990s. Outlook was incorporated into an office suite that included Microsoft Word, Microsoft Excel, and Microsoft PowerPoint. Today, these are not only tremendously used, but also have become the modus operandi of corporate America. However over the years, my computer technology and my tastes have changed so I am recommending some of the other programs I use.

Apple Mail—In 2004, I changed my computer technology from a Dell notebook to Apple iMac and then to MacBook air while traveling. Because I utilize over seven e-mail accounts, I found that some of the products were not able to handle the numerous accounts. I changed in 2007 to Apple Mail and I have not looked back. Apple Mail or Mail as it is commonly called is an e-mail client included with the operating systems OS X and iOS by Apple. Originally developed by NeXT as NeXTMail, a part of their NeXTSTEP operating system, it eventually became Mail after Apple's acquisition of NeXT. The robust client-server software supports POP, IMAP, SMTP, Gmail, Exchange, iCloud, and Outlook. I highly recommend this, if you use Apple computer technology.

Microsoft Outlook—Microsoft Outlook is the de facto standard for most corporate enterprise environments. This robust software completely integrates into the Microsoft family making it quite easy to attach and send and receive documents that are of Microsoft format. One additional feature that I absolutely love is the ability to conduct an e-mail mail merge. You simply type a letter into Microsoft Word and integrate that with your database collected in Microsoft Excel and WhaLa your mail is sent instantly to hundreds if not thousands of clients.

Microsoft 365—In the last several years, technology has altered tremendously allowing many software companies to utilize something known as the cloud. The cloud is nothing more than server-based technology that relinquishes the need to have specific software downloaded to your computer. One simply needs to have an Internet connection and they can gain to databases, e-mails, customer relationship management systems, and even document sharing systems wherever, whenever, and however they need access. For many of you reading, you might recall the days when attempting to download versions of Microsoft suite of product seemed to take forever. And, the costs are significant to Microsoft in terms of distribution and intellectual property maintenance. Like many other firms, Microsoft has made the decision to utilize the cloud to save cost on software development and application. As such, the Microsoft suite of products is available online and in the cloud and currently known as Microsoft 365.

Gmail—Developed by the tremendously successful search firm Google in 2004, Gmail is perhaps one of the first cloud-based e-mail services available to the general marketplace. Gmail allows support for any computer because it is an Internet-based communication tool that only uses Internet browsers as the front end. The robust client-server software supports POP, IMAP, SMTP, Gmail, Exchange, iCloud, and Outlook. I highly recommend the use of Gmail, as it is available on smartphones, tablets, and any computer around the world.

Customer Relationship Management—Aside from the telephone, customer relationship management is the most important tool for any selling professional. Simply put, customer relationship management is either software or cloud-based technology that allows organizations and representatives to organize, automate, and synchronize potential and existing buyers into one database. Selling professionals are then able to manipulate data from a customer in a myriad of ways to understand either phases of the sales process, potential products to be sold to the selling professional, organized sales reports, organize follow-up activity for clients, and even generate invoices. Undoubtedly, selling professionals would not be able to operate in an efficient fashion if not for having good customer relationship management software.

Sales Force—I have used many different types of software in my 31 years of career as sales professional and it all started with a very small yet popular one known as ACT. Eventually, the company was purchased by Salesforce and is now part of the salesforce.com family. Salesforce.com is the preeminent provider of customer relationship management software in the world. From small businesses to large hierarchical enterprises, salesforce.com is the preeminent provider for selling professionals. Over time, the company has migrated to a cloud-based approach so that the software is available on a myriad of devices. It is rather easy-to-use tool and one that most selling professionals cannot afford to be without.

Leads—when I discuss migrating through the sales channel, the first place to begin is with a lead. Lead is an individual that you suspect would be interested in your product or service. And, the heart of every single selling professional is looking for leads daily. There are myriad ways to do this such as networking, looking in regional periodicals, or even watching the news. However, technology has certainly taken over and nowadays it is much easier to find individuals that you might want to do business with a point and a click. So the following tools are being offered to you to assist you in finding leads electronically:

LinkedIn—This is one of the oldest social networks to still be surviving in an exceedingly competitive marketplace. Facebook started it all but the next largest social network is LinkedIn. The services used mostly by business professionals seeking to form alliances with old business partners, groups of similar types of individuals, and prospective clients. LinkedIn only offers availability by connectivity if you have previously done business with the individual or you need to be introduced by someone who has. Resolutely, there are well over 350 million users, with 107 million of those in the United States, yet the service reaches over 200 countries. If you are an individual seeking to do business with other professionals, then LinkedIn is your soul conductivity tool.

Twitter—Twitter is a free social networking microblogging service that allows registered members to broadcast short posts called tweets. Different from something such as Facebook where individuals can post lengthy diatribe and personal opine, Twitter users are obligated to only 140 characters. Therefore, suites are exceedingly succinct but can be read by anyone and everyone around the globe. The value of Twitter is that individuals post updates for news related information, so if you're seeking to uncover information about an organization or person—Twitter is the place. There are approximately 302,000,000 Twitter subscribers today which do not operate like Facebook or LinkedIn. Anyone and everyone can connect. I have found this an invaluable tool because of the short amount of information, but I can discover about prospective individuals.

Google Maps—There is a rationale for having Google maps embedded into a lead generation tool. Google Maps allow me to understand where the business is located and what the operating hours are. If I am seeking to cold call or at least send information, I can quickly understand their location and hours of operation.

Rapportive—Rapportive shows you everything about your contacts right inside your inbox. What I really like about this particular application is that it allows you to understand everything about your contact within an e-mail window and anything your organization might conduct with the client is there as well. This is a great application if you are seeking to have one place to arrange both your e-mail and contact information without having to open separate customer relationship management and e-mail accounts.

Boomerang—In this class, I am offering you a tool that operates exceedingly well with Gmail. Boomerang allows you to schedule messages to be sent or returned at a later date. Not every e-mail package allows you to do this and I find it exceedingly helpful if I don't want to send an e-mail automatically. Most importantly, there's no charge and it connects to one of the strongest e-mail packages in existence.

Documents—No matter the type of computer you're using or should you desire to utilize a tablet, you will always need to have a document package in order to send a quick letter to a client, provide a price quote, or most importantly a proposal. Therefore, I am recommending the following document packages to make life systematically easier:

DocUsign—This is an incredible service that started roughly three years ago. DocUsign actually takes documents that you have converted into an Adobe acrobat format and makes them available online so that the client can review and authorize signature. This cloud-based software is amazing because it saves on printing, postal mail, and awaiting someone to authorize a document. Clients have used this for wills, mortgages, and a plethora of other legal documents. If you are looking for an easy way to get a signature on a proposal or contract, then this application is a must.

Google Docs—With the increase of cloud-based technology in 2013, Google has decided to enter the market in order to assist their present and future client base. Similar to the Microsoft collection of products or even the Apple collection of products such as pages, sheets, keynote, Google Docs provides a similar suite of software products. Without having to purchase any software whatsoever, a sales professional has the availability of producing spreadsheets, proposals, and even presentations online. The only requirement would be a good browser and an available Internet connection. Most individuals love the price—free! So if you're looking for an exceedingly useful way to get access to an office suite of products without having to pay for, then Google Docs should be in your toolkit.

Microsoft Office—Similar to what I mentioned earlier in this chapter about Microsoft Outlook, Microsoft Office suite of products whether downloaded individually or as Office 365 is the de facto standard for most corporate organizations in the United States. The easy use of Microsoft Word, Microsoft Excel, Microsoft PowerPoint, Microsoft Access, Microsoft OneNote, and Microsoft Outlook provide an exceptionally easy interface for windows-based, Mac-based, or tablet users. Additionally, Microsoft Office is available on most tablets and smartphones that operate the android operating system or the Apple OS system. Most of you reading this information probably already have access to Microsoft Office, so there's no need for acquisition. But if you don't have anything and are seeking to go with the king of content development and amalgamation, then Microsoft Office must be in your toolkit.

News—I was exceedingly fortunate growing up as a kid because my grandmother always read a newspaper. I took my fascination of current events from watching her read from front to back page daily. She read everything from the *New York Post*, the *Daily News* to the *New York Times* and she did so without hesitation. The important point to understand about news is that you need to have a good foundation of current events to carry forth provocative conversations with economic buyers. You have to be in the know! Therefore, you should make it a point to have read and reviewed either paper-based or electronic news daily. If you fail to understand what's happening in the world around you, then you are failing your clients and cheating yourself. With that in mind, I'm providing you some of the most widely available resources for discovering useful information for cocktail, business, and personal conversation:

Mashable—This is a digital media site that begun in 2005. Most of the information on Mashable concerns technology and technology-based products. I find this an exceedingly useful resource to discover new tools that I can use in my sales day or quite simply information that I can share with clients.

BuzzFeed—This is another digital media service that amalgamates content from around the world. BuzzFeed will take content from the world's leading newspapers, magazines, media outlets, and public relations institutions and place relevant content into a digital feed. If you want to make your presence felt, then this is an application that you must have on your desktop or on your mobile device.

Flipboard—This is another digital media service that amalgamates information from your social media sources as well as media outlets around the world. The interesting notion about Flipboard is that everything is under one roof, but almost reads like a newspaper throughout the day. For example, you might be reading news from the *New York Times* and you see an update for one of your Facebook friends in another "article." If you're looking for an interesting way to read the news as well as keep updated on all things around the world then this is a must for your toolkit.

Google Alerts—Google Alerts are e-mail updates of the latest relevant Google results (web, news, etc.) based on your queries. Follow client or prospect organizations, and receive an e-mail when they're in the news. Depending on the amount of news, you may need to refine your queries.

Wall Street Journal—Simply put, there is no other financial periodical around the world. If you are selling to other businesses then you must be reviewing and reading the *Wall Street Journal* daily. Review the front page for current information related to politics and economics and then review the marketplace section on all things related to business. Every single CEO as well as anyone in the financial services business has the *Wall Street Journal*. If you are serious about selling then you must be serious about reading and reviewing the *Wall Street Journal*.

Bloomberg—One of the largest competitors News Corp. and an organization embedded within every major financial institution, Bloomberg, is the media giant when it comes to business-related information. Most media outlets rely on Bloomberg for access to Wall Street and global markets. The organization has websites and a host of video services for subscribers to gain access to important financial and business information. This is something that also must be in every salesperson's toolkit.

Reuters—This is a 100-year-old institution that began its roots in Europe and has grown exponentially around the world. Reuters provides information on current events, global politics, global economics, and general news-related information. All the firms have historical roots in Europe; there are freelancers and writers around the globe providing instant access to world-related information.

Video—I started my career in sales in 1982 and at that time, telephone was the only way to communicate with individuals. The only way to illustrate products and services was directly visiting the clients. Today, telephone services and even video communications have increased the capability to be with potential clients wherever they are. Most importantly, video enables selling professionals to record something, upload it to a particular service, and allow thousands if not millions to view that content. Here are some of my favorite services for selling:

YouTube—According to statistics, there are roughly 1,000,000 loads of video per day on YouTube. And, just as many people search YouTube for content, as they would use Google to discover general information. I utilize YouTube to provide content-related information to prospective and existing buyers. I find the service to be absolutely invaluable for positioning my content, my personality, and my presence. And, the use of video enables the broadcaster to speak directly with potential subscribers as if they're in the room with them. One of the best examples is the wine connoisseur Gary Vaynerchuk who started to use YouTube as a method of selling more wine and his Queens liquor store. Today, he is a social media entrepreneur because his videos gain over 1 million views per session!

Vimeo—If YouTube is an astounding service for hosting video, then Vimeo is an exceedingly close competitor. The service has well over 100 million actively available uses of the service and 22 million subscribers. It is an incredible competitor to YouTube and one that should not be avoided.

SlideShare—This is an absolutely amazing tool that began its roots with LinkedIn and has now developed into its own niche. The tremendous thing about SlideShare is that if you have a Microsoft PowerPoint or Apple keynote presentation that you would like to record and show the world then SlideShare becomes an invaluable resource. This is an amazing tool to be used for product demonstrations, product announcements, or other content-related methods such as training sales or even customer service professionals. This is one you cannot do without.

Appointments—I know about you but the way of the world is having several appointments so that you can move throughout the day from one prospective client to another. There are a number of tools such as Microsoft Outlook, iCal, and even Google calendars. However, each requires the individual subscriber to schedule an appointment with another individual. A few years ago, I found one incredible tool that is a must for your sales toolkit:

Time Trade—Integrates easily with enterprise sales, marketing, service, customer relationship management, and business process management systems to accelerate bottom line business results and drive inbound sales, while enhancing customer experience and loyalty. The most fascinating thing about this particular tool is that it is not only cloud-based, but it also integrates completely with any calendar tool on the market today! Yet, the most important thing is that it places all the control in the hands of the prospective or existing client. They simply view your calendar online and make an appointment based upon your availability! My calendar has increased in activity by 54 percent simply by utilizing this tool. You still utilize your existing calendar but you must have this on a website or blog so that your prospective clients can get access to you. If I have mentioned before other items that must be in your toolkit, then this is a must must must!

Note Taking—Taking notes is an invaluable tool for any selling professional. Aside from a notepad, there are a few electronically available products that I think you might want to take a look at:

Microsoft OneNote—If you do a lot of note taking, attend multiple meetings during the week, and collaborate with others on projects, then Microsoft OneNote packages everything under one roof. Rather than look for multiple pages or have in your possession multiple manila files, Microsoft OneNote allows you to place everything under tabs so that you can have anything and everything you need on one device at one time. What makes this application exceedingly helpful is that it's available on most mobile devices and computers. Forget your smartphone at home? Then open up your laptop or workstation startup Microsoft OneNote and all of your notes are available to you.

Evernote—Somewhat similar to Microsoft OneNote, the Evernote family of products help you remember and act upon ideas, projects, and experiences across all the computers, phones, and tablets you use. Depending upon the type of tablet device, you can actually utilize your own handwriting, use the keyboard, or attach pictures and e-mails from other applications. I find Evernote similar to Microsoft OneNote to be very a helpful resource in organizing my day and time.

Tech Tools—There are a number of technology tools that you should always have at your disposal, so I want to briefly mention just a few of these:

Cellular Phone—As a selling professional, you need to be available to prospective clients at all times. Selling is a 24 hour a day, seven days a week profession. Not many would agree with me, but if you want to be on the top prong of the sales profession then you need to be accessible. Providing your cell phone number to prospective and existing clients and allowing them to reach you on and off hours will make you an invaluable resource among the competition.

Paper—Unless you're incredibly good at text messaging and fumbling through the multiple ways of keying information on a mobile device, or are able to do without a laptop and begin typing a message or taking notes, it is always best to have a small pad by your side. I have purchased something known as Moleskin notepads over the years and find them invaluable tools. I have them in several sizes but the one I use most often is approximately the size of a pocket wallet. I place one on my breast pocket, one on my nightstand, and one on my desk. I always have access to paper so that when a client calls and I need to make a short notation I always have something available.

Good Pen—If clothes make the man then a good pen makes him look like a king. You should always have a very good brand name pen at your disposal. I tend to use a Pelican, Mont Blanc, Krone, and Tiffany. When you want to sign the most important deal ever then you need to have a good pen.

iPad or Tablet—Smartphones and tablets have become the way of the world. They have eclipsed the use of paper-based systems and to a certain extent even laptop and computers. If you want to be in touch with your prospective and existing clients in a myriad of ways then a tablet will allow you to do so very conveniently.

Web Meetings—There are a growing number of companies that are making incredible use of web conference. Since the recession of 2007, many American organizations have sought to reduce expenses in travel and productivity and web conferencing is the answer. In short, web conferencing is the equivalent of a meeting in video but conducted over the Internet. Web conferencing saves time since individuals do not have to travel for face-to-face meetings, it saves expenses on hotel and air, and increases productivity so that participants can share and interact with the screen displays. Web conferencing makes it exceedingly easy for individuals to connect for one-on-one meetings, sales teams to connect that work virtually, or organizations to conduct an array of training. Given a good application and a good Internet connection, you can bring teams of people together instantaneously.

GoToMeeting—Perhaps one of the most notable sources for online meetings, GoToMeeting allows individuals instantaneous access while using cloud-based technology. Individuals from a myriad of locations and using a variety of technology devices can connect with each other. This includes tools such as smartphones, tablets, personal computers, and Apple-based OS X computers. The interesting thing about GoToMeeting is that it is incredibly easy to use and allows individuals to interact online utilizing things such as a whitespace, polling, and the ability to text message. This is a fee-based service, but does make it very easy for selling professionals to connect with representatives and clients.

FreeConferenceCall.com—This is an incredibly valuable service for the soloprenuer or entrepreneur that is desirous to save money. I have used FreeConferenceCall.com for a number of years on the telephony side and have just switched over to its web hosting services. This is incredibly useful if you want to record a webinar, a training application, or even a product demonstration. The service quickly and easily records everything on your desktop in a high-density format and makes it instantly available for download and viewing once completed. Not only is it free, but is also incredibly easy to use.

WebEx—An application sharing and conferencing service that is widely used for presentations, demos, training, and support from WebEx Communications. Everything that the presenters see and manipulate on their computers can be viewed by everyone in the conference. The application is very similar in design to GoToMeeting and allows multiple individuals to be brought together instantaneously. Similar to GoToMeeting, the service works on a variety of applications and I should point out you can even schedule meetings similar to the way that you would schedule a face-to-face meeting in visiting with the client.

Skype—If you are seeking an application through which you can speak with people from all over the world without having to worry about large phone bills or transmission, then Skype is your application. Although I have a voice over Internet Protocol (IP) line, I find Skype incredibly easy to use and exceedingly proficient in speaking with global clientele. A number of my freelancers in India and Australia use Skype to connect with me daily. I find this an invaluable tool that I need to have.

LogMeIn—I am certain that there have been plenty of times where you wanted to operate at a destination not located near the client. LogMeIn is a cloud-based screen sharing service that allows you and another user to share screens. Used mostly by technical representatives for training and for quality assurance, I have found LogMeIn equally effective with illustrating important documents, spreadsheets, or even PowerPoint presentations. When you have people located abroad and want to illustrate instant information by showing them a process visual utilizing your iPad, then LogMeIn is a great choice.

Join.Me—Similar to LogMeIn, Join.me is a fairly new service that also allows screen sharing. I have found this exceedingly effective with one-on-one clients. And most importantly, the price is exceedingly appealing. The service is very easy to use because you simply invite people to join you through a special access code, so there is no need to worry about security. If you're looking for an inexpensive alternative for screen sharing, especially when it comes to demonstrations or PowerPoint presentations, this is a great application.

Apps—With the use of cloud-based technology and the plethora of smartphones on the market today, I just wanted to briefly mention how the use of apps can help your day operate more intuitively and less painfully. Similar to the manner in which I use software applications on my computer when I'm in the office, I tend to use a number of apps so that I can quickly communicate with prospective and existing clients. Some of them are as follows:

USA Today—This allows me quick access to current event news.

Text message—This allows me to quickly send a message to my prospective or existing clients should I be running late to a meeting or there tends to be too much traffic.

Cloud magic—A very interesting e-mail application that allows me to send and receive e-mail updates.

Microsoft OneNote—As discussed earlier.

Dropbox—A cloud-based filesharing service that allows me to have accessibility to every file on my system, wherever I go.

Spotify—A boy always needs to listen to good music throughout the day to reduce the stress level.

Nike+—It allows me to keep track of everyone while I'm on the go, especially when I'm moving from hotel to hotel.

Skype—As discussed earlier.

World Clock—Allows me to access the current time of any global city so that I know when to communicate with particular parties in their current time zone.

Daylite—A Mac OS-based application which is my customer relationship management system.

Falcon expenses—Keeps track of all of my expenses such as mileage, dry cleaning, and parking.

Nextiva—This is the voice over IP system that I utilize in my office but is also available as a soft phone on my smartphone.

I also want to point out some additional items that all good selling professionals should have at their disposal so that they are more successful throughout their sales day period:

Read openly about selling—No matter where you are and what you do, you should always be conscious about the profession that you're in and how you can serve and support your present client base. I am always reading about my competitors, the industry, and alterations in the industry. This allows me to be on top of my game and continually service my clients with the best value possible. No matter what you do, you should always be taking classes or reading new material in the sales profession.

Read openly about your industry—You need to make a habit to constantly read about the industry that employs you. Understanding the political and economic challenges allow you to become more malleable in serving your clients better. The more you learn about your industry, the better you are able to obtain competitive information in order to aid new clients.

Read openly about your competition—Just as important as your industry, you really need to understand your competition. I'm a former track athlete and while I did not acutely focus on the competition, I was exceedingly aware of what they did and what they had that made them just as relevant as I. Learning the idiosyncrasies, differentiation will aid you in creating more value for your client as well as positioning your services more keenly in your client's direction.

Website—It goes without saying that in some industries and organizations it may be exceedingly difficult to have your own website. Yet, if you are seeking a way to gain new leads and bring more attention into your world, then it would be exceedingly beneficial to create your own website. This is not a website that is self-gratifying, but rather one that offers the value of your services and how you need other individuals. It should also list a myriad of ways to contact you and things that you have done such as case studies and testimonials that have helped other clients.

Blog—In addition to website, you might want to develop your own blog. These web-hosted sites allow you to post personal opinion, objective information, and even valuable information to those within your demographic reach. Blogs are a wonderful way of expressing how you can help others. For example, if you were the selling representative for printing company, you might want to blog about new types of printers coming out into the market and even some interesting things about new three-dimensional printing.

Podcast—If you find that writing is not your bailiwick but seem to be able to express your views in a very conversational tone then podcasting may be an opportunity for you. Podcasting is nothing more than utilizing your tablet or computer to speak similar to a radio show and offer valuable content to your listeners. If you're seeking to gain good example of podcasts, you might want to view some of the ones that I've developed on iTunes or simply view some of the listings within the service.

VidCast—If writing and speaking like a radio show host is not your thing but you want to produce some type of content, then you might want to try VidCast. Similar in design to a podcast and utilizing either your smartphone or tablet device, you can record a short video of a particular topic and then have that hosted either on YouTube or Vimeo to be viewed by others. Individuals have posted things about craft beer, knitting, how do they use certain software applications, or even a lecture about sustainability for social enterprise. No matter the topic, you are certainly able to grab leads from producing original content that your demographic will be interested in.

LeadPages.Net—And, if you're looking for a very good method and inexpensive alternative of not only attracting leads, but also converting them into clients, sometimes building a webpage is a nightmare. This is a wonderful service that actually has template websites prebuilt so that people submit their name and e-mail address so that you can capture that into a database. I find this service absolutely invaluable to my business because I can grab leads very effectively. In fact, my lead generation increased by 78 percent just by using their services.

Additional Resource Books and Websites

The following annotated resources are here to provide you with tools for lifelong learning. A track is a continuous circle and so is learning. Education is a daily must for a sales professional.

Books

- Barron, R. 1998. *What Type Am I*. New York, NY: Penguin.

  This is a wonderful book that assists you with personality assessment. This book will help you learn more about you and help you build rapport with clients.
- Blanchard, K., and S. Bowles. 2001. *High Five*. New York, NY: William Morrow and Company, Inc.

  Once again, Ken Blanchard knows how to motivate the individual for his or her best performance. *High Five* provides wonderful techniques and principles to help take your selling to a new level.

- Blanchard, K. 1993. *Raving Fans*. New York, NY: William Morrow and Company, Inc.

    This Blanchard work is yet a classic to help you build creative alliances with your customers and prospective clients. Use the techniques and watch your relationships be better for it.

- Carlson, R. 1997. *Don't Sweat the Small Stuff*. New York, NY: Hyperion.

    Riding the sales roller coaster gets obscene. Dr. Carlson illustrates how to smooth out the issues of the day and let you focus on important issues not trivial.

- Carnegie, D. 1936. *How to Win Friends and Influence People*. New York, NY: Pocket Books.

    Anyone worth their title and business card must read this perennial classic from the selling master. In fact, anything Carnegie should be the mantra for most selling professionals. Read Carnegie and you will be better for it. Read this book and learn more about you and relationships than you ever imagined.

- Carnegie, D. 1944. *How to Stop Worrying and Start Living*. New York, NY: Pocket Books.

    Another classic from Carnegie and a great one at that! This work illustrates how to compartmentalize the most difficult calls and issues to make a better day and a better life.

- Godin, S. 2003. *Purple Cow*. New York, NY: Penguin.

    Targeted more for the marketing professional, this book includes useful techniques for a selling professional. One of the best is "Be remarkable"—leave a lasting impression for higher levels of sales and service.

- Hill, N. 1960. *Think and Grow Rich*. New York, NY: Fawcett Crest.

    A classic motivational book, written by Napoleon Hill and inspired by Andrew Carnegie, it was published in 1937 at the end of the Great Depression. The text is founded on Hill's earlier work, *The Law of Success*, the result of 25 years of research based on Hill's close association with a large number of individuals who managed to achieve great wealth during the course of their lifetimes. This is a must read for the spirited selling professional wanting to achieve new levels of success!

- Mandino, O. 1968. *The Greatest Salesman in the World.* Hollywood, FL: Fell Publishing Company.

  The *Greatest Salesman in the World* is a classic guide to the philosophy of salesmanship. A parable set in the time just prior to Christianity; the book illustrates the 10 principles for selling success. Written more as an inspirational story, the book might confuse due to implication but definitely worth the read.

- Mandino, O. 1975. *The Greatest Miracle in the World.* Hollywood, FL: Fell Publishing Company.

  This is another classic by Mandino. The ending is a surprise and yet very motivational. If you are seeking a great pick-me-up, this is the one!

- Parinello, A. 1994. *Selling to Vito.* Holbrook, MA: Adams Media Corporation.

  Looking for a new method to get into see the decision maker, this is the book for you. Good techniques and advice.

- Peale, N.V. 1956. *The Power of Positive Thinking.* New York, NY: Fawcett Crest.

  The widest read self-help book of all time. You will get positive motivation from this book and you will view the world differently when you conclude. This is a must for the lone selling professional who frequently gets down on himself or herself.

- Robbins, A. 1991. *Awaken the Giant Within.* New York, NY: Summit Books.

  Awaken the Giant Within covers a wide range of topics, from goal setting, to Neuro-linguistic programming (NLP), personal finance, and relationships. A large book and not a classic but adapts well to Generations X and Y.

- Whiting, P. 1947. *The Five Great Rules of Selling.* New York, NY: McGraw Hill Book Company.

  A classic book on selling, this is the book that got Dale Carnegie and Associates started. The book contains a formula for those just beginning selling as well as a great review for the advanced representative. This is a must read for all groups and one that you must have in your library for easy reference.

- Ziglar, Z. 1985. *Secrets of Closing the Sale*. New York, NY: Berkley.

  Similar to Dale Carnegie, Zig Ziglar is a master of selling success and a wonderful individual. Zig illustrates through the art of persuasion how to effectively thwart objections to close sales quickly.

  Audio Products

- Tracy, B. 2002. *The Psychology of Selling*. Minneapolis, MN: Nightingale-Conant.

  Brian Tracy lays a 12-point goal-achieving method for reaching whatever destination you choose in life, how to "program" yourself for success, which products are best for you to sell, how to "read" your prospect's needs, and how to overcome objections, and how to motivate 99 out of 100 potential customers to buy. He is a bit monotone, but most people investing in the profession listen to Brian.

- Tracy, B. 2002. *The Psychology of Success*. Minneapolis, MN: Nightingale-Conant.

  Recorded similarly to *The Psychology of Selling*, provides a 12-point blueprint for peak performance and high achievement. The recording is also very monotone yet offers great goal setting techniques for those who want to be high achievers.

Newspapers and Magazines

- *The Wall Street Journal*
  200 Burnett Road, Chicopee, MA 01020
  (800) 568–7625

In order to know your client and your prospective customers, you must remain in line with the news and ahead of the competition. The *Wall Street Journal* is the premier source of business, industry, and financial information. Make this a part of your daily reading. An online subscription is also available.

Associations

- Toastmasters International
    PO Box 9052
    Mission Viejo, CA 92690
    (949) 858–8255

Toastmasters offer a proven way to improve your communication skills. By participating in a fun and supportive Toastmasters group, you'll become a better speaker and leader and gain confidence to succeed in whatever path you've chosen in life. This is a great venue if you fear making presentations to one or more people. Toastmasters will build your confidence.

Book Summary and Action Steps

There is nothing here that is an absolute must from anything that I posted within this chapter. I tend to use a lot of tools to help support a number of different efforts in my sales day. Since I'm doing a lot of the attracting, converting, and retaining from a solo perspective, I tend to utilize a number of different tools to make my day less stressful. There is no rhyme or reason of what I've chosen but I have 31 years of experience in researching and reviewing an array of products. I'm neither endorsing nor suggesting that you obtain all of those I've mentioned in this chapter. I do suggest that you obtain just a few so that you are focused on the most important thing that you need to do through out your sales day—generate leads and close business. If even one of those tools can help increase the effectiveness by over 50 percent then you have hit a grand slam. My desire is that you go out each and every day collecting as many leads as possible so that you are the most successful rap in your organization.

Ideally, you would've read this book chronologically so that each chapter had built upon itself to provide you with enough information so that you made some subtle changes to become a better selling professional. No one said it was going to be an easy road ahead and no one said that you weren't going to have hurdles in your path. The reason why I developed this book is because there has been a tremendous amount of training and support for today's sales agent. This is a profession I deeply admire as it is my passion. And, I want selling to be your passion. But you cannot have that passion and you cannot have that success without having the proper tools come to the proper confidence and the proper processes to eliminate many of those hurdles so that they become speed bumps. My role in providing you with this book is to help you navigate through today's contemporary issues such as customers having more information and changes in consumer behavior so that you can understand how to create more value and rise above the competition. The notion today is to create as many relationships as possible so that you can illustrate your value, your differentiation, and how you benefit the customer. By utilizing the ideology of what's in it for me for the customer, you will become more successful by focusing on your most important asset—the customer. They know the products and services you sell, they know about your company, and they have done a side-by-side analysis of your services versus your competition. Now, it's your job to illustrate how your relationship will create the tangible and intangible value in conducting business with you and your organization.

The easiest path to success is finding the key economic buyer who makes the decision. The least path of resistance is building an extensive network of leads and referrals so that you never have to make an initial call to someone unknown. And, the best methodology is creating a series of processes and tactics that attract people to you. The tools, the techniques, and the processes illustrated in this book will help you eliminate all of the gaps that you faced and will help you to the sell in this new norm. The tipping point today is challenging you to create some changes in your sales day so that you can be a better selling professional tomorrow. I wish you the very best of luck and God bless you and the opportunities that will come to you by the changes you've made.

August 23, 2015

Other Works by Drew Stevens PhD

Books
Magnetic Leadership
Split Second Selling
Split Second Customer Service
Split Second Leadership (coming Fall 2009)

Booklets
Grand Slam Customer Service
Little Book of Hope
Meetings with Muscle
Pump Up Your Productivity
Sales Acceleration – Overcoming Selling Mistakes
Solving the Productivity Problem

Audio Cassettes, CDs, Albums
Developing Employee Performance Plans
Grand Slam Customer Service
How to Negotiate Anything
Little Book of Hope
Power Managing
Presentations with Power
Pump Up Your Productivity
Split Second Selling Audio Course

Seminars and Workshops
Split Second Selling Master Class
Sales Leadership Course
Pump Up your Productivity
Inside Track to Self Mastery
The Winner in You

Newsletters/Podcasts
The Sales Strategist
Make it Happen

Templates for Selling Professionals

Clean up Database

Every six months to one year it becomes vital to remain atop your client database and maintain some cleanliness. Customer Databases can become quite large, cumbersome and most importantly outdated. The best advice is to send an email or succinct letter to a client/prospect alerting them of your intent to update important account information. Suggest to them this will only take a few moments and is impetrative in assisting you to maintain contact.

Letter Form

Dear _____

I am hopeful that all is well with you. I am grateful that we had the opportunity to connect the other day. Pursuant to our conversation, I am sending this note to assist me in updating your account profile.

At your convenience would you please review the current information and indicate where necessary any changes. I am particularly focusing my efforts on your email, your current address and contact telephone numbers.

Please do not underestimate my gratefulness of your time but this is a great exercise to ensure we do not lose contact.

Kind Regards,

Email Format

I am sending the following email to let you know that I am in the process of performing my annual database maintenance. In an effort to ensure I have the most current information I am seeking a few moments of your help.

At your convenience would you please review the current information and indicate where necessary any changes. I am particularly focusing my efforts on your email, your current address and contact telephone numbers.

Please do not underestimate my gratefulness of your time but this is a great exercise to ensure we do not lose contact.

Kind Regards,

Closing Questions

Every sale requires a focus on client value and customer appreciation. Additionally, each sale is contingent upon not only how well the selling professional has moved the client relationship closer but most importantly has the representative fit the need with the product or service. Good questioning skills are required to help the representative understand client's desires. II is important to lead a sale down a path to assist both sides in gaining closure. The questions on the preceding page provide a pathway to your success.

1. How would your superior make a similar decision?
2. Do the terms and objectives meet with your approval? If so what is the best manner to proceed?
3. Who is the person responsible for allocating funds and resources?
4. When will the appropriate person or you approve this project?
5. What is the impending event?
6. Who are the influencers?
7. Who are the recommenders?
8. What is the decision process and who is involved?
9. If you could buy today without worry of price or circumstance, would you make the purchase?
10. What is the budget for this type of purchase?
11. Why are you buying/looking?
12. If you proceed how will this improve the organization?
13. How might this service or project improve your competitive position?
14. When might be the appropriate time to begin this project?

Cold Calling Fitness

The art of cold calling is serious business. And not many like to do it, however there will be times when it is necessary. Cold Calling requires patience, persistence and professionalism. The trick is to remain constantly positive and vigilant. More important, you must remember that cold calling is meant to generate leads - just relationships! Too many of you reading this believe that when you cold call you are to sell something, this is far from the truth. Whether stocks, insurance or any other product the idea behind cold calling is to begin a relationship.

The comedian Jeff Foxworthy uses a moniker with every joke that states, "You might be a redneck if". Before you read each of the ten tips say to yourself, "You might be a cold calling nuisance if..."

1. You pick up the telephone and have no idea who you are calling. Someone called me recently and asked for the proprietor. Know whom you are calling.
2. After hello you begin with chitchat. Speak with conviction and have a purpose for every call.
3. You call and have conversations with gatekeepers. Call only decision makers. Stop wasting time with gatekeepers that are paid to detain you. Research the person you want to reach before you pick up the phone.
4. You do not know anything about the business or industry you call. I had a gentleman call me this morning to sell me a copier without an iota of knowledge of my business. Imagine the shock when he discovered I was a sales trainer.
5. Start your call with information about your company. Begin your call with a purpose and a value proposition. If you cannot articulate the value to the recipient do not make the call.
6. Begin your calls with inane questions. Questions such as "How you doin'" is for Joey Tribiani from the series Friends. Unless you desire a data dump comparable of being in a therapist office, stop. If you want conversation then speak articulately.

7. Operate each call without a clear purpose. Use a checklist for each call and have a path. A call should have a beginning, middle and an end.

8. Get over the myth that you are calling to sell something. NO YOU ARE NOT. You are simply calling for an introduction and to gain an appointment, any other reason is a mistake on your part.

9. You fear rejection. Get over it. Lead Generation whether you conduct it for your business or other complex organization is about the rejection business. In order to be successful get out of your comfort zone and deal with it.

10. Commence from call to call. I know of an organization that requires representatives make over 50 calls per day. This is unrealistic. What should be measured is not the call volume but the calls that lead to appointments. Success is should be measured by quality over quantity.

Here are the steps and techniques necessary for cold calling:

10 Steps

1. State your name
2. State the name of the suspect for verification
3. Provide a very brief statement for your call
4. State a reason for your relevance based on current events
5. Raise a question of interest based on a need for clarification and interest
6. Provide your value proposition to the prospect
7. Use a pithy testimonial congruent to the prospects issues
8. Assess the interest and create some action
9. Develop an actionable step such as another telephone call or direct appointment
10. If there is a lack of interest proceed with a question for a referral in another division or department
11. Remember to thank the prospect and confirm any actions
12. Evaluate the call and make notes for the next meeting

Sample Template to follow:

1. My name is _____
2. I am calling to speak with _____
3. I am with Stevens Consulting Group. We specialize in sales productivity and business growth.
4. I understand that XYZ is seeking more efficiencies with its sales talent and better closing ratios. Am I correct with that?
5. I am under the impression that there is a need to provide some productivity investments in staff based on a recent Wall Street Journal article.
6. Would it be of interest to discover how you can increase profits and production without raising head count?
7. We found that working with _____ that this is a key issue for them and has improved their efficiencies over 35%,
8. Would you be interested in learning more about this?

9. Let me suggest I send some materials and follow up with you on Thursday 21 June at 10:30 AM EDT. Would that be convenient for you?

10. Thank you for your time and I look forward to speaking with you then. I will also send to you by courier a complete press kit and links to some valuable information on the web that will assist you in preparing for our next call. Again thank you for your time and enjoy the remains of your day.

Customer Service Follow Up

Peter Drucker one wrote that the focus of every organization is the customer. The customer is the essence of products, market research and most importantly customer service is why the firm exists. 98% of most companies lose focus with customer service, it becomes and afterthought and an excuse or sometimes an interruption. Customer Service is your business lifeline and failure to review, focus and implement systems that build on customer relationships will negatively impact business.

Customer Service Letter

Dear Susan:

I was recently notified of your Customer Service issue. Please note that the essence of our business is complete client satisfaction. I am in contact with our team presently working to follow up and determine not only the reasons of the issue but to find an immediate resolution. Once I finalize the information I will respond to you with closure.

Thank you for your patronage and ability to serve you. Please note the value of your service and the importance of the relationship.

Kind Regards,

Drew Stevens

Customer Service Pledge for all Clients

1. The customer is the most vital aspect of my business.
2. The customer does not interrupt my day, they are the integration of it.
3. Nothing happens in the business without proper customer service.
4. Customers that smile and enjoy the service become marketing avatars.
5. Customers that allow us to exceed expectations inform others of our humble nature.
6. Networks grow because of content customers.
7. Customers own our brand.
8. Customer to Customer influences are strong, remain one with the customer.
9. We exist to match customer wants and needs, our ideal is to satisfy.
10. The best compliment for any customer is a referral.

Follow Up from Networking Event

It is imperative after meeting new colleagues and peers at an association or other organization function to send them a quick thank you for the acquaintance. Sending a card, (not an email) a physical card makes the meeting memorable as people do not typically place such tresures into the garbage. Thank you cards a wonderful methods to express not only gratitude but differentiation.

Follow Up from Networking Letter

Dear Deborah:

It was a sincere pleasure to meet you and Barry on 20 September 2009 at the IMC event in St. Charles. I was very intrigued about your conversation on business performance and would welcome the opportunity to meet again and further our discussion.

I am enclosing my business card and complete contact information. However, my plan is to connect with you again on 5 October 2009 at 9:30 AM CDT. I look forward to speaking with you again.

All the best

Drew Stevens PhD

Follow Up Letter

Never conduct a sales meeting, or any other customer presentation without a proper follow up to any telephone call or direct meeting. Individuals today are simply too busy and there is too much clutter creating less memory recall and event importance. To help you and to continue to move the process you must orchestra all activities with the client. The first begins by creating actionable items using a series of written correspondence to help. ***Do not send an email,*** make yourself different by using paper based letters sent through postal mail or other resources such as Send Out Cards.

Follow Up Letter Template

Dear Robert:

It was a pleasure to speak with you on Tuesday 30 September 2009. I most appreciated the conversation and the time spent discussing the productivity issues you mentioned.

Pursuant to our discussion, I am forwarding to you the article I mentioned on Closure Ratios for Selling Professionals along with a summary of he conversation.

My plan is to call you on Friday 3 October at 11:15 AM EDT to discuss your objectives and determine the possible metrics to help meet those objectives. If this is not a convenient time, would you mind providing me some alternatives through any of the contact points offered in this letter.

I look forward to our next conversation.

Interview Questions

Lets face it no one remains at a job forever. More importantly many selling professionals walk into job interviews – unprepared. The point of an interview is to make a first impression in a split second!

I recall a young woman I interview in 1995. She walked into my office with three manila folders. Each folder contained vital information that she was prepared to ask me. I was so impressed I hired her on the spot.

Interview Questions

Company

1. I reviewed the company website and discovered three interesting things about the company. They are:

-
-
-

2. Can you tell me how that might affect the future products and services?
3. What is the potential impact to the business in the next three years?
4. How do the present political, environment and technological issues affect the company?
5. What might be the most significant changes to the company in the next two years from a competitive perspective?
6. What are the firm's objectives in the next two years?
7. How might they meet those objectives?

Competition

1. What is the impact of the firm on the competition?
2. How does the current competitor parallel existing business?
3. Given less competition how is the company viewed within the industry?
   a. How do its products and services assist with that attitude?
4. What is this firm's secret weapon against the competition?
5. What changes are happening to align and surpass the competition strategically?

The Work

1. What are issues that assist in helping employees remain productive and competitive?
2. What support is provided to personnel to assist them with immediate productivity?
3. What are the strategic and visionary principles that are integrated into the environment?
4. How does the company manifest that culture?
5. How does the company allow its employees to remain competitive?
6. How does it measure its success?

Introduction Letter

The most imperative part of any selling professional is creating an articulate perspective to introduce the company and its products and services.

If your firm is having issues retaining clients or acquiring new ones and you are seeking strategic methods to optimize selling effectiveness, we can assist!

> "It is such a technology, fast-track driven business industry that we are in today Drew Stevens quickly understands your issues and reaches out to find immediate and productive results!"
>
> —Pat Schaumann, CMP, CSEP, DMCP

As a manager and business professional do you ponder?

- How to increase productivity amongst staff
- How to decrease client attrition
- How to gain assistance from Marketing to optimize selling
- How to create ambassadors throughout the organization?

Does your organization need:

- Efficiencies within your work teams
- Acquisition of new clients with less capital
- Communication strategies

Your firm will obtain:

- Enhanced communication and appreciation of work teams
- Creation of selling efficiencies for quicker profits
- Increase communication for effective customer service

Since 1997, Drew Stevens PhD has assisted organizations world wide to dramatically accelerate business growth. Drew is a well-known speaker; author and consultant that works personally and collaboratively to immediately gain results.

Call 877-391-6821

Our simple desire is to quickly improve your condition. We establish objectives, and metrics with
Our services include:

- Strategy – Discover things the competition cannot
- Customer Service – Create an experience not an event

- Communication – bridging the generational enigma
- Sales Skills – Creating value and allure that increases the bottom-line
- Marketing – Using the power of customer loyalty to evoke effective marketing

COACHING

Every elite athlete or business leader has a coach or mentor, someone to be accountable to and someone who can give a fresh perspective to a situation. Coaches provide an inside track and keep you in the game-mentally and physically. Coaches assist with competitive threats and assist in maintaining and increasing motivation.

If you want to grow your business and continually improve your service to clients, then you should request a coach. Our Individual Coaching Program is not designed to be passive. The aim is for you to get very involved in helping you achieve amazing results.

Our setting is a unique opportunity for you to meet privately and candidly to share ideas that assist with increasing profitability. You will learn to avoid mistakes and capitalize on good ideas. You gain Key Performance Measures (KPM) at each meeting so that like an athlete you move forward with accountables.

Drew Stevens has coached hundreds around the world, they trust Drew's opinion and respect his judgment. They get confidence from his record of accomplishment of business growth, leadership, and practical advice. More importantly, they get results.

Since 1988 Drew Stevens PhD has been exclusively focused on helping business, improve their growth. Drew...

- Has done extensive research on motivational theory and understands how to maintain momentum in challenging times.
- Worked with several well-known multinationals since 1984, he has sold, has led, and comprehends your deepest challenges.
- Has delivered speeches, workshops, and seminars at more than 700 strategic marketing and business growth events worldwide since 1993.
- Has written countless articles on how high performing firms operate.

- Has written several books on marketing, customer service, and how to dramatically accelerate business growth.
- Has developed products, methodologies, and leading training programs in four separate businesses that still operate successfully today.
- Currently coaches over 100 business professionals to help them achieve high levels of success.
- Drew Stevens is one of the leading Top Selling Professionals in the world. Drew entire business career has focused on competitive intelligence, business growth, and strategy. He quickly understands the issues that drive, accelerate, and help maintain business success.

Please call Drew Stevens through the contact form of this website or at 877-391-6821 and get business results now!

Index

OTHER TITLES IN OUR SELLING AND SALES FORCE MANAGEMENT COLLECTION

Buddy LaForge, University of Louisville and Thomas Ingram,
Colorado State University, Editors

- *Creating Effective Sales and Marketing Relationships* by Kenneth Le Meunier-FitzHugh and Leslie Caroline Le Meunier-FitzHugh
- *Lean Application in Sales: How a Sales Manager Applied Lean Tools to Sales Processes and Exceeded His Goals* by Jaideep Motwani and Rob Ptacek
- *Improving Sales and Marketing Collaboration: A Step-by-Step Guide* by Avinash Malshe and Wim Biemans
- *Key Account Management: Strategies to Leverage Information,Technology, and Relationships to Deliver Value to Large Customers* by Joel Le Bon and Carl Herman

Announcing the Business Expert Press Digital Library

Concise e-books business students need for classroom and research

This book can also be purchased in an e-book collection by your library as

- a one-time purchase,
- that is owned forever,
- allows for simultaneous readers,
- has no restrictions on printing, and
- can be downloaded as PDFs from within the library community.

Our digital library collections are a great solution to beat the rising cost of textbooks. E-books can be loaded into their course management systems or onto students' e-book readers.
The **Business Expert Press** digital libraries are very affordable, with no obligation to buy in future years. For more information, please visit **www.businessexpertpress.com/librarians**. To set up a trial in the United States, please email **sales@businessexpertpress.com**.